The
Reincarnation
Mystery Revealed

The Reincarnation Mystery Revealed

Dr. H.M. Munje

Bahá'í Publishing Trust
6 Canning Road, P.B. No. 19
New Delhi-110 001
INDIA

FIRST EDITION 1997

ISBN: 81-86953-02-7

Typeset at Pagitek Graphics, Laxmi Nagar, Delhi-92 and
printed at Divyanshu Graphics, Tel.: 5752195, 5764330

CONTENTS

PREFACE

From 1940 onwards on my frequent visits to interior villages in India, I came in contact with the masses who had believed for ages in reincarnation; predestiny by God for every soul; the caste system and many other related ideas and practices. Similar beliefs were observed in the cities.

At that time I conceived the idea of writing articles on these topics for the enlightenment of the masses. This I wanted to do with strong support from their religious scriptures, common sense, and a scientific outlook. An article on reincarnation was prepared in Hindi and it was published much later in *Abhá Magazine* in four instalments.

When I wrote it in English, completing the work on February 26, 1950, it assumed the size of a small book. Now it is enlarged.

In pursuit of my investigations over the years, I very carefully studied the widest possible range of Hindu sacred literature related to the subject—both in Sanskrit and translations into other languages. Translations of the Hindu Holy Scriptures from Sanskrit into English vary considerably. In fact, some translations contain words and phrases that are not given or not intended in the original Sanskrit at all. Therefore, in some cases I have made my own translations, following the letter and spirit as closely as possible and endeavouring to be accurate. In other instances I have used translations by Dr. Bhagwan Das, a very prominent author and Theosophist, as I find these to be of high quality.

I have gratefully used some appropriate references from Dr. Raymond A. Moody's books, *Life After Life and Reflections on Life After Life.*

Reincarnation is a highly complex, subtle, deep and difficult subject. The reader will note that certain themes and statements arise repeatedly. Each time they are investigated from a new angle.

God has blessed the human soul with mercy, compassion, love, and other tender and beneficial attributes. Yet it has been observed that belief in the theory of reincarnation and metempsychosis sometimes prevents a person from helping someone else who is in need or in peril. The believers in reincarnation at times, look coldly at persons in real trouble. They think that such troubles and afflictions are due to the sins of the victims' past lives and hence they should not interfere. Let them suffer and burn away their evil deeds of their previous lives. Their souls will be unburdened and they will be prepared for a better life in their next birth. In my view, this kind of belief has slackened the development of divine attributes in some communities and has retarded the desired progress of the nation as a whole.

A sudden and sharp squeal of a mortally hurt dog was heard from the roadside. Patients sitting in my clinic in Bombay rushed to the window to see what had happened. I also peeped out of the window. A dog was crushed under a truck and some passersby were gathering around the bleeding dog which was breathing its last. They felt pity toward the dying animal. Some seemed angry at the truck driver, but he did not care at all. He started the truck with a jerk and was gone. My feeling of compassion was aroused.

One middle-aged person who was sitting outside my clinic was absolutely unconcerned. He said to me, "Why do you waste your precious time on such a thing, doctor? The dog must have killed the driver in Purva Janma (past life), so it got its punishment. Why should we bother about it?" This gentleman, as I knew him, was otherwise a noble, religious, pious and honest person, but his belief in reincarnation had made him hard-hearted and merciless.

Another time the telephone rang and I was called for a critical cancer case. As I was politely taking leave from other waiting patients for this emergency, one lady accosted me, "Why do you take up such terminal cases? After all, there is no cure for cancer. Why do you spoil your good name by helping such an incurable patient? Don't you know that cancer is a divine scourge for the expiation of the sins of his past life?" Due to her belief in reincarnation she did not care at all if the patient suffered or died! But by the grace of God that cancer patient got well and lived long thereafter.

During the Second World War, on hearing a rumour that several thousands of people were killed in gas chambers in Germany, one staunch believer in the theory of reincarnation exclaimed: "Look at the justice of God! Yama Raj—the Angel King of Death—is chastising people who had sinned in their previous births!"

Even today, some dogmatic believers in the law of karma, and reincarnation think that when terrorists kill apparently innocent persons, the terrorists are in fact repaying their victims who must have tyrannized them in past lives. Could this cold-blooded, irrational attitude be due to some or the other misunderstanding derived from their belief in reincarnation?

Dr. H.M. Munje

INTRODUCTION

What happens to the human body after death is clear to all. It is either burnt to ashes or it decomposes and returns to the earth. But, is this the end of the human being? Or is there something more? This is the question which each person has to answer for himself.

To any thoughtful person it is clear that a life of three scores and ten, or a little more, or a little less, on this planet cannot be the ultimate achievement of millions of years of evolution — It would be fruitless, illogical and therefore quite unthinkable for an intelligent Creator. The infinite perfections of this universe clearly point to a more fitting conclusion to millions of years of development and evolution. Therefore there must be a higher purpose to life than just existence!

Each of the religions of the world emphasize that life continues even after the death of the body. They cite the fact that each person does not get his due reward or punishment during the course of his life on this planet as proof. Thus some form of the human being, the soul, must continue so that justice, mercy, compassion and love may be fulfilled.

In this book, Dr. Munje clarifies the Scriptural and spiritual reasons for a rational belief in life after death. The Hindu Scriptures are essentially accepted to be the Vedas, the Srimad Bhagwad Gita, and the Manu Smriti. The Puranas, the Upanishads, and the other Writings are the sayings of various Holy persons, often with the Vedas as their base. The Ramayana and the Mahabharata have a standing as historic epics/religious literature. In fact the multiplicity of beliefs that constitutes Hinduism makes it difficult to cite a common acceptance of what is Scripture and what the sayings of various holy persons. This problem has been partly resolved by Dr. H.M. Munje in this book by the use of quotations from a large variety of sources including the Vedas, the Manu Smriti, the Srimad Bhagwad Gita, the Mahabharata, the Ramayana and the Upanishads. Such an extensive perusal of Scriptural literature adds to the authenticity of this much needed work.

Dr. Munje's insight into the subject arise from his deep knowledge of both the Bahá'í and Hindu Scriptures. The Bahá'ís believe in the oneness of God, oneness of religion and oneness of mankind. To them, the purpose of their lives is to know and worship God.

The Avatar clearly states the Divine Truths. He reveals an appropriate plan for the development of the individual and society. He teaches man how to make progress in all fields of human endeavour. His teachings are enshrined in His Holy Book and are passed on as the standard for His era.

Viewed in this light the Scriptures of all the religions conform in common belief and are united in their expression of spiritual reality. If this book was to achieve only this that it causes people to realise that all the Scriptures come from one common source, i.e., God and agree on basic Spiritual teachings, it would have achieved a great deal.

All the religions of the world are part of a great plan of God. They all await their Messiah who is to come and unite them and all mankind. In a very convincing way Dr. Munje has emphasised that God's Avatar has come, and it is a challenge to every person to investigate this claim and accept Him. It is upto mankind now to realise that the solution to the existing chaos is available. We have to arise and fulfil the progress of civilisation on this planet through global unity. Then will the purpose of the prophecies of the past be realised and Vasudeva Kutumbha Kum will be established. The whole world is but one country and mankind its citizens.

CHAPTER ONE

Religion, science, and human reason go hand in hand. By the grace of God, science progresses through conscientious human efforts, whereas revealed religion advances age after age through a new and fresh revelation from on high, through God's Manifestations (Ishwara Avatar).

Religion, science and reason are complementary tools used by man in his constant search for a deeper understanding of reality and his desire to attain salvation. In the words of the blessed Lord in the *Gita*:

ज्ञानविज्ञानतृप्तात्मा कूटस्थो विजितेन्द्रियः ।
युक्त इत्युच्यते योगी समलोष्टाश्मकाञ्चनः ॥

[गीता 6: 8]

"He who is well contented with knowledge and science is called a yogi, the conqueror of senses, he for whom iron, rock and gold are the same."

[*Gita VI, 8*]

इदं तु ते गुह्यतमं प्रवक्ष्याभ्यनसूयवे ।
ज्ञानं विज्ञान सहितं यज्ज्ञात्वा मोक्ष्यसेऽशुभात् ॥

राजविद्या राजगुह्यं पवित्र मिदमुत्तमम् ।
प्रत्यक्षावगमं धर्म्यं सुसुखं कर्तुमव्ययम् ॥

[गीता 9:1, 2]

"To thee, the uncarping, verily shall I declare this most profound secret. Having knowledge of Nirguna Brahma along with the knowledge of manifest Divinity, knowing which you will be free from the evil of worldly existence. This knowledge is a sovereign science, a sovereign secret, supremely holy, most excellent, directly enjoyable, attended with virtue, very easy to practise and imperishable."

[*Gita IX, 1, 2*]

The fundamental principles of all true revealed religions are one, as their source is God Himself. Hinduism, Zoroastrianism, Buddhism, Christianity, Islám, the Bahá'í Faith, and other religions are all one in essence. In the words of Bahá'u'lláh, the Founder of the Bahá'í Faith, believed by Bahá'ís to be the Manifestation of God for our age.

"The purpose of religion as revealed from the heaven of God's holy Will is to establish unity and concord amongst the peoples of the world; make it not the cause of dissension and strife. The religion of God and His divine law are the most potent instruments and the surest of all means for the dawning of the light of unity amongst men. The progress of the world, the development of nations, the tranquillity of peoples, and the peace of all who dwell on earth are among the principles and ordinances of God.

Religion bestoweth upon man the most precious of all gifts, offereth the cup of prosperity, imparteth eternal life, and showereth imperishable benefits upon mankind."

[Bahá'u'lláh, *Writings of Bahá'u'lláh*, p. 235]

"That the divers communions of the earth, and the manifold systems of religious belief, should never be

allowed to foster the feelings of animosity among men, is, in this Day, of the essence of the Faith of God and His Religion. These principles and laws, these firmly-established and mighty systems, have proceeded from one Source, and are the rays of one Light. That they differ one from another is to be attributed to the varying requirements of the ages in which they were promulgated."
[Bahá'u'lláh, *Writings of Bahá'u'lláh, p. 310*]

Hence, should the followers of any two religions advance two interpretations or understandings about the same fundamental principle, some misunderstanding may occur between these followers; yet, the religions themselves are not in conflict because they are all from the same divine source.

Similarly, science can not contradict religious truth, as that truth is in conformity with reality—and both science and religion reveal reality to man. In the words of 'Abdu'l-Bahá, the son of Bahá'u'lláh.

"Any religious belief which does not conform with scientific proof and investigation is superstition, for true science is reason and reality, and religion is essentially reality and pure reason; therefore, the two must correspond."
['Abdu'l-Bahá, *The Promulgation of Universal Peace, p. 107*]

Science is a product of the human mind. It is influenced by divine revelation in each age. Human beings have been granted free will by the grace of God. They do things voluntarily and spontaneously. Hence, scientific knowledge and achievements may be misused. True religion provides the guidelines so that scientific developments can be beneficial to humankind.

Simultaneously, scientific discoveries can confirm knowledge available through divine revelation but not clearly understood up to that time. How, then, can religion oppose science or science, religion?

Scientists and religionists may differ in their opinions. This is not bad or unnatural. "From the clash of opinion the spark of truth comes forth." Since they both strive to attain the same goal — to achieve an understanding of the nature of reality — they ultimately express the same truth. Science uses scientific method, involving trial and error, but revealed religion in its pure form has no element of error. In the latter case, humans must develop their capacities to understand the newly revealed truth. This requires a change of attitudes. A rigid adherence to old viewpoints is characteristic of a static, unchanging society making little progress where the masses are being led to perdition.

Thus, there is no harm in verifying religious beliefs and theories in the light of science. For this, scientific strides must be properly channelised. This will ensure the progress and development of the whole human race.

In India, itself, people, who have taken scientific and materialistic approaches to life and living do not believe in reincarnation or at least have serious doubts about it. There are others who believe in reincarnation. They extend various theories as follows:

(1) A human being may be reborn as a human being only.

(2) A human being may be reborn as a human being or as an animal.

(3) A human being may be reborn as a human being, as an animal, a tree, or even a stone.

(4) A human being may ultimately or even immediately attain moksha (liberty) and does not return.

Most people believe in reincarnation as the theory of karma (law of action). By this they mean that the form in which they return is the fruit of the actions of their previous life. Such post-Vedic views are taken for granted by nearly all the Hindu sects and philosophical schools.

The fact is that the theory of reincarnation and transmigration of souls has over the centuries raised doubts, contradictions and dilemmas that are hard to resolve.

We cannot find any belief in reincarnation and the transmigration of souls in the [Veda Samhitas] or the *Brahmana Granthas*. In the Vedic religion, the next life is spiritual. Some souls ascend after death to the heavenly world while others go to the depths (hell). The doctrine of rebirth appears in the orthodox Brahmanical tradition only later, at the time of the Upanishads, although, arguments against the theory of reincarnation can also be derived from a study of the Upanishads — a good example of apparent contradictions found in Hindu holy writings.

Although most Hindus interpret passages from the Gita and certain other Hindu holy writings in such a way as to support their belief in reincarnation and transmigration, we shall demonstrate in this book that interpretations of many of the same passages can be set forth questioning and doubting that belief.

Therefore, these beliefs obviously need to be investigated in light of both modern science and religion. During the course of this study, conclusions might be reached contrary to some peoples' age-old impressions. Those with investigating minds can overhaul their views when new insights and deeper understanding is achieved. Particularly if they realize that the old, untested beliefs were and are harmful to society. Therefore, this writer humbly and ardently appeals to all concerned to be just and fair, and to be loving and compassionate in their heart of hearts.

Slow or fast, a forward march is in the nature of things. The natural law never admits any retrovertive movement of life or retrograde living process.

Every moment past is past once and for all, never to return. Every action performed can never become unperformed. Life can never move backwards.

A wheat plant cannot ever be reverted to the selfsame wheat seed from which it grew. The ground wheat flour can never make a retrogressive life movement and become the wheat seed once again. The ground wheat flour can never be wheat grains once again.

Can a ripe but bitter fruit cut off from the tree be put back to the flower state and be forced to spring forth again as a sweet and delicious fruit the second time? No!

Can an unschooled and unlettered mature man be made a child again by a retrogressive process in order to school and educate him? No! Once he has passed the stage of childhood he cannot be brought back to it to educate him. Adult education is possible, but making him a child again is impossible. That stage in his life is passed forever.

Can any and all combined forces on earth reverse an 80 year old bachelor to a young blooming man of 16 in order to get him married? Certainly not. He can marry all right, but cannot become a young man for that purpose.

Isn't it unscientific and illogical even to think of a comeback process, in nature and through this process expect a progressive result of evolution, improvement, refinement, purification and the like?

There is no retrogression, no revertive movement in nature at all; neither in time or space; neither in living or inanimate objects. 'Abdu'l-Bahá declared:

"When the shell is opened, it will be apparent and evident whether it contains a pearl or worthless matter. When the plant has grown it will bring forth either thorns or flowers; there is no need for it to grow up again. Besides, advancing and moving in the worlds in a direct order according to the natural law is the cause of existence; and a movement contrary to the system and law of nature is the cause of non-existence. The return of the soul after death is contrary to the natural movement and opposed to the divine system."

"Therefore, by returning, it is absolutely impossible to obtain existence....."
['Abdu'l-Bahá, *Some Answered Questions*, p. 329]

Why is the return of the soul after death opposed to the divine system? Firstly, we should consider the view that the physical world is in perfect correspondence with the spiritual world and that both the physical and spiritual worlds are in the divine system.

"The worlds of God are in perfect harmony and correspondence one with another. Each world in this limitless universe is, as it were, a mirror reflecting the history and nature of all the rest. The physical universe is, likewise, in perfect correspondence with the spiritual or divine realm. The world of matter is an outer expression or facsimile of the inner kingdom of spirit."
['Abdu'l-Bahá, *The Promulgation of Universal Peace, p. 270*]

Similarly we find in the *Atharva Veda*:

सनातनमेनमाहुरुताद्य   स्यात्   पुनर्णवः ।
अहोरात्रे प्रजायेते अन्यो अन्यस्य रुपयोः ॥

[अथर्ववेद **10, 8, 23**]

"He is called the Ancient, He again cometh new today; (similarly) day and night are being generated, (this and that are) semblances of one another."
[*Atharva Veda X, 8, 23*]

Secondly, both divine and natural laws are persistent. Even if we try to resist, eventually we must follow them. There is no going against the laws of God, either natural or supernatural.

Thirdly, both in the material and spiritual worlds the law of life is upgoing (urdhvagah). In the *Mahabharata* it is written:

उपरिष्टाटसो लोको याऽयं स्वरिति संज्ञितः ।
उर्ध्वगः सत्पथ: शश्वद् देवयान चरोमुने ॥

[महाभारत, स्वर्गारोहण पर्व, 3, 21]

"O Muni! That which is called the lofty favorite realm is much exalted. The onward movement for attaining to that realm is elevatory. Hence it is known as the urdhvagah (upgoing). That is the right path, the excellent way. Only the divine vehicle can carry the soul to that destination."

[*Mahabharata, Swargarohan Parva, 3, 21*]

It follows that re-entry into any immediate or remote past stage is an impossibility in the flow of life. Within a stage there may be ups and downs, humps and bumps until the end of the onward march within that stage, but once the boundary line is crossed, there is no passage or process of returning, and the next stage is on a higher level.

A person may become fat or emaciated, gladdened or saddened, educated or left ignorant, wealthy and healthy or poor and diseased, spiritually developed into a saint or corrupted into a devil, but every moment his upward flow of life continues; he never reverts downward to his previous age life. Similarly, once he is physically dead he can never be brought back to his physical life, either in the same body that he left at the moment of death or in any other body composed of physical elements of matter.

The spirit of man, after his material death, passes on to the spiritual world which is a step forward in the spiritual lives of individuals. This same truth is expressed in *Shrimad Bhagwad Gita*, the Holy Song of the Lord:

देहिनोऽस्मिन् यथा देहे कौमारं यौवनं जरा ।
तथा देहान्तरप्राप्ति र्धीरस्तत्र न गुह्यति ॥

[गीता 2: 13]

"Just as the dweller in the body has childhood, youth, (and) old age, following the same way he gets a different body; the wise do not get deluded thereby."

[*Gita II, 13*]

In this holy verse, there is no mention of the soul's coming back to this corporeal world once again and obtaining some earthly body composed of material elements. On the contrary, the statement unfolds the ever-progressing stages in the life of the soul. From being related to the childhood-body the soul proceeds to the youth-body; from the youth-body, again the soul proceeds to the old-age-body, and so on. The soul can never go back to any of the preceding stages of its life after having proceeded to a higher stage each time. After youth, childhood can never return. Similarly, after old age the soul cannot go back to the youth body. In the same way after physical death the soul enters into the spiritual world. How can it, ever again, wear any physical body composed of material elements? Life proceeds on and on. How can it twist its onward course into a retrograde movement, against the laws of nature, either divine or material? 'Abdu'l-Bahá said,

"......*Advancing and moving in the worlds in a direct order according to the natural law, is the cause of existence; and a movement contrary to the system and law of nature is the cause of non-existence. The return of the soul after death is contrary to the natural movement and opposed to the divine system.*

Therefore, by returning, it is absolutely impossible to obtain existence; it is as if man, after being freed from the womb, should return to it a second time. Consider what a puerile imagination this is which is implied by the belief in reincarnation and transmigration. Believers in it consider the body as a vessel, in which the spirit is contained, as water is contained in a cup; this water has been taken from one cup and poured into another. This is child's play. They do not realise that the spirit is an incorporeal being, and does not enter and come forth, but is only connected with the body, as the sun is with the mirror. If it were thus, and the spirit by returning to this material world could pass through the degrees, and attain to essential perfection, it would be better if God prolonged the life of the spirit in the material world, until it had acquired perfections and graces; it then would not be necessary for it to taste of the cup of death, or to acquire a second life."

['Abdu'l-Bahá, *Some Answered Questions*, *pp. 329-30*]

The forward development of the soul is referred to in other holy verses in the *Shrimad Bhagwad Gita*:

वासांसि जीर्णानि यथा विहाय नवानि गृह्णाति नरोऽपराणि ।
तथा शरीराणि विहाय जीर्णान्यन्यानि संयाति नवानि देही ॥
नैनं छिन्दन्ति शस्त्राणि नैनं दहति पावकः ।
न चैनं क्लेदयन्त्यापो न शोषयति मारुतः ॥

[गीता 2: 22-23]

"As a man casting off worn out garments takes on
other new ones, likewise the embodied (soul),
casting off worn out bodies, goeth on to others
that are new. Weapons cannot cut it nor can fire
burn it; water cannot drench it nor can wind
make it dry."

[*Gita II*, 22-23]

The above sacred verses, do not indicate that a soul
makes an about turn to reinhabit this material world
which it has left behind after its physical death. Nor
does the soul re-enter the same or another physical
body.

On the contrary, these verses elucidate the qualities
of the soul which is non-material, and cannot be cut by
weapons, or burned by fire, or drenched by water, or
dried by wind. The other world is not composed of
material elements; it is spiritual. That kind of spiritual,
non-material body is specifically described in the following Shlokas from the *Mahabharata*:

तेजसानि शरीराणि भवन्तय त्रोप पद्यंवाम् ।
कर्म जान्येव मौदगल्य न मातृपितृ जान्युते ॥
न संस्पदो न दौर्गन्ध्यं पुरीषं मूत्रमेव स ।
तेषां न चरणो वस्त्रं बाधते तत्र वै मुनै ॥

[महाभारत, स्वर्गारोहण पर्व, 13-14]

"O Moudgalya! Their bodies have a glorious brilliancy which is awarded for their pious deeds. They are not composed of mother's ovum and father's sperm.

O Muni! Those bodies never sweat nor smell obnoxiously nor even have they any urine or faeces. Also their clothes never become dusty."
[*Mahabharata, Swargarohan Parva, 13-14*]

In the same vein 'Abdu'l-Bahá has written:

"......*In the other world the human reality doth not assume a physical form, rather doth it take on a heavenly form, made up of elements of that heavenly realm.*"
['Abdu'l-Bahá, *Selections from the Writings of 'Abdu'l-Bahá, p. 194*]

This is not only true for those with good deeds but also for the evil ones. In the *Yajur Veda* the point is obvious:

असुर्य्या नाम ते लोका अन्धेन तमसावृताः ।
ताँस्ते प्रेत्यापिगच्छन्ति वे के चात्महनो जनाः ॥

[यजुर्वेद **40: 3**]

"The evil ones, namely those wrapped in deep blind error, go after death to the worlds beyond, and even those people who kill their own selves (their own consciences)."
[*Yajur Veda XL, 3*]

This indicates that the ones who knowingly and deliberately sin and the other evil ones who remain in

deep blind error and go on sinning by habit, both go to
the same world beyond this earthly world.

The next world is different from this world. There we
reap the fruits of our actions performed in this world.
Evidences of this is given in the following two Shlokas
from the *Mahabharata*:

इह यत् क्रियते कर्म तत् परत्रोय भुज्यते ।
कर्म भूमिरियं ब्रह्मन् फल भूमि रसौमता ॥

[महाभारत, अरण्य पर्व 3, 247, 35]

"Whatever actions are done in this world the
same are reaped in that world, O Brahman (the
one informed of divine knowledge). The divine
view is this: this is the action-world and that is the
fruit-world."

[*Mahabharata, Aranya Parva, 3, 247, 35*]

तत्रापि सु महाभाग: सुख भागभिजयते ।
न चेत् सम्बुध्यते तत्र गच्छत्यधमता तत: ॥

[महाभारत, अरण्य पर्व, 3, 247, 34]

"The fortunate one is born over there with the
share of happiness. If one does not conscientiously do his duty over here, then he goes into the
abject evil condition over there."

[*Mahabharata, Aranya Parva, 3, 247, 34*]

Both those who do good deeds and those who do evil
deeds go to the other transcendent worlds (Paraloka).
There exist worlds beyond this material world. These are
quite different from this ephemeral world of water and
clay. God is the Infinite Creator. He has created infinite
worlds. Our minds should therefore not be bound by this

tiny, transitory earth ball on which we briefly live. In the lucid words of 'Abdu'l-Bahá:

"The idea that existence is restricted to this perishable world, and the denial of the existence of divine worlds, originally proceeded from the imaginations of certain believers in reincarnation; but the divine worlds are infinite. If the divine worlds culminated in this material world, creation would be futile; nay, existence would be pure child's play."
['Abdu'l-Bahá, *Some Answered Questions, p. 330*]

The human soul, being eternal, has to live and go on and on, first through the successive stages of physical growth and, after physical death, through the successively progressing stages and conditions of purely spiritual advancement. These various stages of progression have some relationship with the "clothes", the "garments", the "coverings" mentioned above in the *Gita* (*II, 22*) which are connected with the soul and facilitate its constant onward march both in this physical life as well as in its life beyond.

When the child-body is worn out, the soul climbs up to a higher rung of the ladder of life and puts on a youth-body. Ultimately, in this physical life, when its old-age body is worn out, the soul discards the physical body and the physical world as a whole is abandoned. After death the human soul enters into a different world altogether. This is the soul-world the spiritual realm on high, from which there is no return to the physical world. In that spiritual world the human soul puts on abstract clothing suitable to that celestial world. We recall the words of the *Mahabharata*: "Also their clothes never become dusty."

[*Swargarohan Parva, 14*]

Each body is absolutely "new" to the soul in its ever advancing journey of life inasmuch as any state through which the soul passes once is never regained. It is for this that the holy *Gita* specifically uses the word "new" (*II, 22*). This word "new" is quite clear in the sense of "the unprecedented". In the sacred statement of the holy *Gita* (*II, 13*) three successive stages are mentioned in progressive order: (1) childhood, (2) youth, and (3) old age. Each stage is an unprecedented stage for the soul. Similarly, the fourth and next stage necessarily must be a new, unprecedented one. That is the stage of putting on a new kind of unearthly and abstract body. Also, how can the *Gita* (*II, 13, 22*) state that we get "new" "bodies" or "garments" or go through childhood, youth and old age if we return to have physical bodies and garments and stages of life of the same old kind again? We must be reasonable.

In fact, Holy Books of the world's great religions generally teach that the human soul after physical death goes to a spiritual world.

Science definitely indicates that the human body goes on changing during its life on earth. Biology teaches that the process of metabolism comprises two processes that work simultaneously and co-operatively: (1) anabolism and (2) catabolism.

Anabolism is a constructive process within the protoplasm so that food or other material at a relatively low level of complexity becomes more complex until it is finally worked up into living matter. This is how count-less tiny new cells are being constantly formed in the composition of all the tissues of the living body. Each cell has its little span of life and a specific function to perform in the living body.

Catabolism involves the breakdown or decomposition of substances into their simpler constituents. Hence, it is a process of the dying out of the micro-organisms. Cells, having performed their functions, get senile and die.

By the assimilation of food, water, air, heat, rays, and various energy vibrations, the living body grows. Various chemical, radioactive and other processes of life occur within the tissues of the body to produce its growth and enhance its vital energy. At the same time, through various excretions, exhalations, emission of energies and vibrations, and the discharge of stools, urine, sputum, vomit, sweat, blood, leucorrhoea, pus, bile, etc., count-less cells are constantly eliminated from the body.

This is how a newly born child weighing 6, 8 or 10 lbs. gradually grows into a big man weighing 125, 150 or even 200 lbs. or more. This body may be reduced in weight but never in age. A young man may be equal in weight to a child but cannot become a child. Old age may be called a second childhood but actually and physi-cally it is not.

We also see that the human soul is connected with various progressive embryonic bodies or "garments" in the womb of the mother, the zygote, segmentation, morula, blastula, gastrula, neurula to foetus until at last it is born in the form of a baby. Within two years or so, all the tissue cells are gradually changed and new cells compose the body of the child. The same soul remains. Again at the age of seven years or so, another body that is connected with soul is gradually composed of new cells. A similar but progressive process takes place and, in a further eight years or so, all the new cells take the place of old and worn out ones and compose a new young body. Then at the ages of 21, 36 (or 40) and 50 (or 60) and so on, almost all the body cells are changed each time. But throughout this changing of the cells and bodies the human soul remains the same, acquiring different experiences and witnessing new and ever-progressing phases of physical life. This can be what the Hindu Holy Scriptures mean by successive "reincarnations" through which the human soul passes in this earthly life.

The fact that the spirit unfolds in three stages through three "births" is described and elaborated upon in the *Aitaraya Upanishada* in the following way. The *Shruti* says:

पुरुषे हवा अयमादितो गर्भोभवति यदेतद्रेतः तदेतत्सर्वेभ्योऽङ्गे भ्यस्तेजः संभूतमात्मान्येवात्मानं विभर्ति ।
तद्यदा स्त्रियां सिञ्चत्य थैनज्जनयति तदस्य प्रथमं जन्म ॥
[ऐतरेय उपनिषद् 2: 1]

"At the very beginning the embryo is generated in the man — that brilliant quintessence of all his body limbs held within, which is exactly like him- self — is surely the semen which, when poured, is born (conceived) in the woman, (that) is the very first birth!"

[*Aitaraya Upanishada 2: 1*]

Thus, the *Aitaraya Upanishada* proclaims that there is no previous birth.

तत्क्रिया आत्मभूयं गच्छति। यथा स्वमङ्ग तथा।
तस्मादेवां नहिनस्ति। साऽस्यैतमात्मानमन्त्रगतं भावर्यति
सार्भावयित्री भावपितव्या भवति। तं स्त्री गर्भ-विभीती।
सोऽग्र एव कुमारं जन्मनोऽग्रेऽधि भावर्यति।
स यत्कुमारं जन्मनोऽग्रेऽधि भावयत्यात्मानमेव तद्।
भावयत्येषां लोकानां संतत्यै एवं संतता ह्रीमे लोका:।
तदस्य द्वितीय जन्म॥

सो अस्यायमात्मा पुण्येभ्य: कर्मभ्य: प्रतिधीयते।
अथा स्यायमितर आत्मा कृतकृत्यो वयोगत: प्रैति।
स इत: प्रयन्नेव पुनर्जायते तदस्य तृतीय जन्म

[एतरेय उपनिषद् 2: 2-4]

"That becomes as the woman's own limb... the tissue. It is for this reason that this welcome soul over here does not give pain.

That nourishing lady becometh capable of giving nourishment, and holding the embryo, evolves it before giving birth, she also enhances its progress after that. This way generations increase and the population of all peoples spreads. That is his second birth.

This second soul is made to represent his good deeds. Hence this soul performing duties, having lived his life, journeys away from here for good. Again he is delivered. That is his third birth."

[*Aitaraya Upanishada* 2: 2-4]

Thus, the *Aitaraya Upanishada* proclaims that the soul at the end of this earthly life goes away for good!

Two extremely important points are derived from this passage from the *Aitaraya Upanishada*: (1) there is no previous birth before conception and (2) when a person dies his soul goes away permanently.

Firstly, the indication that there is no previous birth before conception as given in the *Upanishada* is clearly reinforced by the Universal House of Justice, the supreme administrative body of the Bahá'í Faith, in these words "..... *The soul of man comes into being at conception.*" (From a letter of the Universal House of Justice, July 31, 1970, cited in *Lights of Guidance, p. 261)*. The soul of man is an emanation from God. Also as 'Abdu'l-Bahá states:

> ".... *The spirit encircles the body at the beginning of the amalgamation of the elements and natures in the womb; the power of the spirit begins then to appear in the body gradually and successively according to the preparation and capacity to receive that everlasting abundance (of the gifts of the Lord).*"
>
> ['Abdu'l-Bahá, *Tablets of 'Abdu'l-Bahá, Volume 1, p. 157]*

Secondly, the indication that the soul goes away for good after death, as given in the *Upanishada*, is reinforced by 'Abdu'l-Bahá. "....The spirit of man after putting off this material form has an everlasting life...."
['Abdu'l-Bahá cited in *Chalice of Immortality, p. 40*]

> "*As to the soul of man after death, it remains in the degree of purity to which it has evolved during life*

in the physical body, and after it is freed from the body it remains plunged in the ocean of God's mercy.

From the moment the soul leaves the body and arrives in the Heavenly World, its evolution is spiritual, and that evolution is: The approaching unto God."

['Abdu'l-Bahá cited in *Chalice of Immortality, p. 33*]

The soul ultimately attains the presence of God (the Sakshat Paramatma-Darshan). Therefore, after death man's soul goes away from this material world forever.

Let us now further refer to the holy *Gita:*

अव्यक्तादीनि भूतानि व्यक्तमध्यानि भारत।
अव्यक्तनिधनान्येव तत्र का परिवेदना॥

[गीता 2: 28]

"O Bharata (Arjuna)! Beings were unmanifest in the beginning, are manifest in the middle, shall likewise be unmanifest on decomposition. Where comes in lamentation?"

[*Gita II, 28*]

This passage certainly does not seem to support the view that the soul comes back to adopt a material physical earthly body a second time? The manifest corporeal body is composed of material elements that are constantly in movement. This is only an intermediary stage in the ever-onward journey of the individual human soul, between two unmanifest stages. The soul in itself and by itself ever remains unmanifest even when embodied in the series of its physical and manifest garments (metabolism) throughout its earthly life. This is also referred to in the holy *Gita*:

अव्यक्तोऽयमचिन्त्योऽयमविकार्योऽयमुच्यते।
तस्मादेवं विदित्वैनं नानुशोचितुमर्हसि॥

[गीता 2: 25]

"(The soul) is called unmanifest, unthinkable, immutable. Having thus known this, therefore, to grieve is unbecoming."

[*Gita II, 25*]

अथ चैनंनित्यजातं नित्यं वा मन्यसे मृतम्।
तथापि त्वं गहाबाहो नैवं शोचितुमर्हसि॥

[गीता 2, 26]

"O might-armed (Arjuna)! Even if you regard this (soul) as constantly taking birth and constantly dying, still you should not grieve like this."

[*Gita II, 26*]

Has not the Blessed Lord made it clear here that there is no such reincarnation in the sense as it is popularly supposed to be? Because here the Blessed Lord seems to take it for granted for the sake of argument that even if a person believes that the soul takes repeated births and dies again and again on this earth (which is not the fact), this should not be the cause of grief for him.

It is evident, then, that the human soul continues to live after the death of its physical body, in the unmanifest spiritual world, where it is given a suitable "garment" called "Karma-Deha". This "action-body" (Literally: Karma-Deha), which is referred to in the

Hindu Holy Scriptures, will be an absolutely "new" and unprecedented "covering" for the soul in the spiritual realms above. This "action-body" of the soul becomes ready for use by the soul only after the metabolic physical bodies are worn out, completely exhausted and finally discarded once and for all.

After leaving the physical body over here the soul, as a bird from the cage, takes its flight to the heaven of spiritual realms. As for noble and pious souls:

"They enter into a state which, should we only have the eye to see, we would envy and earnestly desire. It is only because we ignore the beautiful and glorious life of the world beyond that we seem attached to our earthly abode and often forget the goal of our very existence here."

[From a letter on behalf of the Guardian to the author, May 14, 1932, cited in *Dawn of a New Day, p. 196*]

'Abdu'l-Bahá gave the wonderful example of the relation of this life to the next life being like the child in the womb. "It develops eyes, ears, hands, feet, a tongue, and yet it has nothing to see or hear, it cannot walk or grasp things or speak; all these faculties it is developing for this world. If you tried to explain to an embryo what this world is like it would never understand.....but it understands when it is born, and its faculties can be used. So we cannot picture our state in the next world. All we know is that our consciousness, our personality, endures in some new state, and that that world is as much better than this one as this one is better than the dark womb of our mother was."

[From a letter written on behalf of the Guardian to an individual, October 8, 1943, cited in *Lights of Guidance, pp. 162-163*]

As for the sinful soul, a series of repentances, punishments, and torments take place in order to "burn away" the evil deeds and thus unburden the soul until at last it attains the presence of God; the ultimate desire of the soul; the final consummation of all its highest aspirations; the supreme goal of its life and of its very existence. Boundless gladness; eclat and exultation; infinite love and rapturous enjoyment; all of the holiest nature, characterise the celestial condition of the liberated soul. This state is called "Nirvana", the Param Moksha, the infinite liberation, the unending satisfaction, the eternal bliss, the supreme salvation. The *Mahabharata* and the *Manu Smriti* say; see how clearly the following verses depict heaven and hell:

तत्रापि समहाभागः सुख भागधिजायते ।
न चेत् सम्बुध्यसे तत्र गच्छत्वंधमता ततः ॥
[महाभारत, अरण्य पर्व, 3, 247, 34]

"The fortunate one is born over there with a share of happiness. If one does not conscientiously do his duty over here, then he would go into the abject evil condition over there."
[*Mahabharata, Aranya Parva, 3, 247, 34*]

अधर्मदण्डं लोके यशोघ्नं कीर्तिनाशनम् ।
अस्वंर्ग्य च परत्रापि तेस्मात्तत्परिपर्जयेत ॥
अदण्डयान्दण्डयंनृ राजा दण्डयाश्रवैवाप्य दण्डयन् ।
अदशो महदाप्नोति नरकं चैव गच्छति ॥
[मनुस्मृति, 8: 127-128]

"He who punisheth in a way not prescribed by religious ordinances meeteth with infamy and disgrace in this world and also doth not gain paradise in the next world. He should, therefore, shun this method outright, by punishing those who do not deserve punishment and not punishing culprits, the king is put to great disgrace and also he goeth to hell."

[*Manu Smriti, VIII, 127-28*]

साक्षी दृष्ट श्रुतादन्यद्द्विबुवन्नार्यसंसदि ।
अवा इग्नरकर्कर्मभ्येति प्रेत्य स्वर्गाज्चहीयते ।

[मनुस्मृति, 8: 75]

"The witness who saith something quite different from what he had observed and heard falleth headlong into hell, and the virtues which he had performed in order to gain paradise in the world beyond are destroyed by this, his act of sin."

[*Manu Smriti, VIII, 75*]

अवाक् शिरास्तमस्यन्धे किल्बिसी नरकं व्रजेत् ।
यं प्रश्नं विलथं ब्रूयात्पृष्ठसन् धर्मनिश्चये ॥

[मनुस्मृति, 8: 94]

"He who bears false witness concerning questions for determination and clarification of religion, goeth with downcast head straight into the darkest of all hell."

[*Manu Smriti, VIII, 94*]

याऽरक्षन् बलीगादत्ते कर शुल्कं च पार्थिवः ।
प्रतिभागं च दण्डं च स सद्यो नरकं व्रजेत ॥

[मनुस्मृति, 8: 307]

"The king who doth not protect well his subject but taketh ugahi, sali, or tax or monthly penalty, that king immediately after his death goeth to the hell."

[*Manu Smriti, VIII, 307*]

यः क्षिप्तो मर्षयत्यार्तैस्तेन स्वर्गे महीयते ।
यस्त्वै श्चंयन्ति क्षमते नरकं तेन गच्छति ॥

[मनुस्मृति, 8: 313]

"The king who despite suffering difficulties himself from the harassed and the unhappy people, forgiveth them, is highly respected and revered in the paradise. He who, being intoxicated by his sovereignty and who is arrogant of his position of authority, forgiveth them not, goeth to hell."

[*Manu Smriti, VIII, 313*]

राजभिः कृत दण्डास्तु कृत्वा पापानि मानवाः ।
निर्मलाः स्वर्ग मायान्ति सन्तः सुकृतिनो यथा ॥

[मनुस्मृति, 8: 318]

"Sinners who, on receiving punishment from the king, thus liberated from sins, become clean, and, like the saints who have done good deeds, go to paradise."

[*Manu Smriti, VIII, 318*]

धनानि तु यथाशक्ति विप्रेषु प्रतिपादयेत् ।
वेदवित्सु ति विक्तेसु प्रेत्य स्वर्गं समश्नुते ॥

[मनुस्मृति, 11, 6]

"He who gives money according to his capacity for the possessors of divine knowledge attaineth to paradise on his death."

[*Manu Smriti, XI, 6*]

एक एव सुहृद्दर्मो निधनेऽप्यनुयाति य: ।
शरीरेण समंनाश सर्व मन्यद्धि गच्छति ॥

[मनुस्मृति 8:17]

"After the death of the body it is only dharm (religion) which goeth along with the soul, and neither relatives nor friends go with it, for all other connections are destroyed on death."

[*Manu Smriti, VIII, 17*]

In the Brahmana Granthas we find that there is judgement for the soul after the death of its body, and its deeds on earth are weighed in the balance and the soul is rewarded or punished to the proportion of its virtues or sins. People living on earth must do self-sacrificing charities and prayers with devotion to God for the liberation of the souls of their ancestors; that is why to die childless was considered a terrible thing.

There are passages in the Hindu Holy Scriptures to support the view that there is no comeback process anywhere or in any way or form throughout the whole course and procedure of human life, right from its very beginning to eternity. The same reality is clearly attested to in the holy *Yajur Veda* as follows:

ये समाना: समनस: पितरो यमराज्ये ।
तेषाँल्लोक: स्वधा नमो यज्ञो देवेषु कल्पताम् ॥

[यजुर्वेद 19: 45]

"The (souls of) forefathers are in the Kingdom of
Yama (the angel of death). Those (souls) are
homogeneous and conscious. They in that world
are capable of humbling and devoting themselves
to the Divine Being."

[*Yajur Veda, XIX, 45*]

This holy verse of the sacred *Yajur Veda* clarifies the
point that both good and evil spirits, after the death of
the physical body, ascend into the realm of Yama (the
angel of death). In that spiritual world all the spirits —
good and evil — resemble one another (as their spiritual
bodies are composed of heavenly elements) just as in
this physical world all human beings — good and bad —
resemble one another in their bodies composed of
physical elements. So also in that world the souls are
conscious of themselves and of one another.

Further, those souls in the spiritual world are living
without material physical bodies. They maintain their
spiritual consciousness and realise many truths of which
they were ignorant in their physical worldly lives prior to
their ascension. Let us immerse ourselves in the inspir-
ing words of 'Abdu'l-Bahá:

*"The mysteries of which man is heedless in the
earthly world, those will he discover in the heavenly
world, and there will he be informed of the secrets
of the truth; how much more will he recognize or
discover persons with whom he has been associated. Undoubtedly the holy souls who find a
pure eye and are favored with insight will in the
kingdom of lights be acquainted with all mysteries,
and will seek the bounty of witnessing the reality of
every great soul. They will even manifestly behold*

the Beauty of God in that world. Likewise will they find all the friends of God, both those of the former and recent times, present in the heavenly assemblage.

"The difference and distinction between men will naturally become realized after their departure from this mortal world. But this distinction is not in respect to place, but in respect to the soul and conscience. For the Kingdom of God is sanctified (or free) from time and place; it is another world and another universe. And know thou for a certainty that in the divine worlds the spiritual beloved ones will recognize one another, and will seek union with each other, but a spiritual union. Likewise a love that one may have entertained for anyone will not be forgotten in the world of the Kingdom, nor wilt thou forget there the life that thou hadst in the material world."

[ʼAbduʼl-Bahá cited in *Chalice of Immortality,*
pp. 46-47]

Consciousness of the soul before and after physical death is a matter with which we must deal. We can see very well that human child born in this earthly world has, right after his conception and then continuing after his birth, no conscious knowledge whatsoever of what he did and where he was in a supposed previous life or how and why he came back to this supposed rebirth in this particular way and in this particular form.

The holy *Gita* says that the human soul "realizes intellectual consciousness of the previous body" after physical death and that this happens "over there" (*Gita VI, 43*), that is, in the world beyond and not this physical world. If we apply the holy verses of the *Gita* to this world, then, human beings generally would "realize intellectual consciousness of the previous body", but it is a fact that almost no human being on earth ever claims, to possess this consciousness. As for those few who make such claims, we can question their truthfulness, as there have been proven examples of fraud. Both the holy *Gita* and the holy *Yajur Veda* (*XIX, 45*) indicate that the human soul retains its consciousness when born into the world of the spirit.

This consciousness is only one of the bounties of the next world. 'Abdu'l-Bahá, states in this connection:

"In the matrix of the mothers we were the recipients of the endowments and blessings of God, yet these were as nothing compared to the powers and graces bestowed upon us after birth into this human world. Likewise if we are born from the matrix of this physical and phenomenal environment into the freedom and loftiness of the life and vision spiritual, we shall consider this mortal existence and its blessings as worthless by comparison."

"In the spiritual world, the divine bestowals are infinite, for in that realm there is neither separation nor disintegration which characterize the world of material existence. Spiritual existence is absolute immortality, completeness and unchangeable be-ing. Therefore we must thank God that He has created for us both material blessings and spiritual graces, outer sight to view the lights of the sun and inner vision by which we may perceive the glory of God."

['Abdu'l-Bahá cited in *Chalice of Immortality*, *p. 113*]

The next world is sanctified from what we call time and place. Time with us is measured by the sun. When there is no more sunrise, and no more sunset, that kind of time does not exist for man. Those who have ascended have different attributes (conditions) from those who are still on earth, yet there is no real separation.

"In prayer there is a mingling of stations, a mingling of condition. Pray for them as they pray for you."

['Abdu'l-Bahá cited in *Chalice of Immortality, p. 114*]

The advanced souls mingle with the Divine Souls, i.e., the souls of the Manifestations of God, Prophets, Ishwari Avatars, Messengers of God, Rishis, Rasuls, etc. in the spiritual world.

In a nutshell, the basic relationship between this material world and the wonderful spiritual world is pinpointed in this sublime statement from the *Mahabharata*:

इहयत् क्रियते कर्म तत् परत्रोय भुज्यते ।
कर्म भूमिरियं ब्रह्मन् फल भूमि रसौमता ॥

[महाभारत, अरण्य पर्व 3, 247, 35]

"Whatever actions are done in this world the same are reaped in that world, O Brahman (the One Informed of divine knowledge, the Brahma-Gyani). The divine view is this: this is the action-world and that is the fruitworld."

[*Mahabharata, Aranya Parva, 3, 247, 35*]

As mentioned previously, science and religion should be employed hand in hand to investigate reality and to throw light on the subject of reincarnation. The mysterious interactions between this physical world and the world of the spirit have been investigated by Dr. Raymond A. Moody, Jr., in his world-famous, best-selling books *Life After Life and Reflections on Life After Life*. It must be pointed out that Dr. Moody's research findings on "neardeath experiences" are similar to other findings throughout the world, including India. After making a survey of much of the literature on the subject and their own study of cases, two medical doctors declared, ".....Although culture-bound expectations do seem to influence these experiences, reports from different cultures also show remarkable uniformities." (Ian Stevenson and Bruce Greyson, "Near-Death Experiences: Relevance to the Question of Survival After Death," *Journal of the American Medical Association, July 20, 1979, p. 266*). Thousands of people have now reported about "near-death experiences" to researchers in various parts of the world, and many books and articles have been written on the subject. These Researchers include psychologists, psychiatrists, cardiologists, nurses, philosophers, and behavioral specialists.

At the time of writing *Life After Life*, Dr. Moody had investigated 150 cases of "near-death experiences", and the experiences he studied fell into three categories:

(1) "The experiences of persons who were resuscitated after having been thought, adjudged, or pronounced clinically dead by their doctors.

(2)   The experiences of persons who, in the course of accidents of severe injury or illness, came very close to physical death.

(3)   The experiences of persons who, as they died, told them to other people who were present. Later, these other people reported the content of the death experiences to him."

[Moody, *Life After Life, p. 16*]

None of them reached the point of no return and came back to tell of it; they experienced "near-death".

Moody found that, despite the fact that no two persons had exactly the same experiences in detail, there was a great similarity among the reports. Fifteen elements occurred over and over again in the accounts. From these he wrote of an "ideal" or "complete" experience that included all the common elements in the order in which they typically occurred.

A man (or woman) is dying and, as he (or she) reaches the point of greatest physical distress, he hears himself pronounced dead by his doctor. He begins to hear an uncomfortable noise, a loud ringing or buzzing, and at the same time feels himself moving very rapidly through a long dark tunnel. After this, he suddenly finds himself outside of his own physical body, but still in the immediate physical environment, and he sees his own body from a distance, as though he is a spectator. He watches the resuscitation attempt from this unusual vantage point and is in a state of emotional upheaval.

After a while, he collects himself and becomes more accustomed to his odd condition. He notices that he still has a "body", but one of a very different nature and with very different powers from the physical body he has left behind. Soon other things begin to happen, others come to meet and to help him. He glimpses the spirits of relatives and friends who have already died, and a loving, warm spirit of a kind he has never encountered before — a being of light — appears before him. This being asks him a question, non-verbally, to make him evaluate his life and helps him along by showing him a panoramic, instantaneous playback of the major events of his life. At some point he finds himself approaching some sort of barrier or border, apparently representing the limit between earthly life and the next life. Yet, he finds that he must go back to the earth, that the time for his death has not yet come. At this point he resists, for by now he is taken up with his experiences in the afterlife and does not want to return. He is overwhelmed by intense feelings of joy, love, and peace. Despite his attitude, though, he somehow reunites with his physical body and lives.

"Later he tries to tell others, but he has trouble doing so. In the first place, he can find no human words adequate to describe, these unearthly episodes. He also finds that others scoff, so he stops telling other people. Still, the experience affects his life profoundly, especially his views about death and its relationship to life."

[Moody, *Life After Life, pp. 21-23*]

Later, after additional investigation, Dr. Moody wrote *Reflections on Life After Life* in which he wrote of several new elements that were reported to him by more than one person who had near-death experiences of extreme duration. These experiences were not as common as the original fifteen. These include (1) the vision of knowledge, (2) cities of light, and (3) a realm of be-wildered spirits.

What Dr. Moody describes in these two remarkable books is in basic agreement with references we have already given that life after death is a spiritual, not a physical, existence. The people who were interviewed by Dr. Moody cannot adequately describe their experien-ces in words. They were, as Dr. Moody puts it, in a "spiritual world", and he uses the term "soul" to describe what they were. The souls were living without material bodies. The souls were "unthinkable" (see *Gita II, 25* above); we cannot in this physical world have a remote understanding of what they are, as words cannot describe them adequately. They were conscious of them-selves and others. Loved ones recognized each other. Love for others still in the material world is not forgot-ten. The life the person had in this material world is not forgotten.

Some, but not all, persons interviewed who men-tioned the phenomenon said they had a non-material "body" but this term really doesn't describe it. Others never claimed they had a "body" at all. Almost everyone that told Dr. Moody of this "body" became frustrated and said, "I can't describe it" or gave some similar remark. (Moody, *Life After Life, p. 43*). Dr. Moody called it the "spiritual body". (See *Gita II, 13, 22-23 Mahabharata, Swargarohan Parva, 13-14;* and 'Abdu'l-Bahá, *Selections from the Writings of 'Abdu'l-Bahá, p. 194,* above). None of them experienced kines-thesis, odours, or tastes while in the spiritual body, but senses corresponding to vision and hearing were reported as existing in the spiritual body. In fact, "seeing" and "hearing' seemed actually heightened and more perfect than in physical life.

[Moody, *Life After Life, p. 51*]

Some of those who had gone deeply into the "near-death experience" recounted that they reached a "border" or "limit" of some kind. In most cases they indicated that they did not go to the other side. Some described what was "seen" or "felt" on the other side, and in all cases this was beautiful, peaceful, full of light, etc. There is no indication whatsoever that what awaited them on the other side was punishment and entry into another physical body.

The experience of these souls was timeless. Time as we understand it was not existent. No place as we know it existed once the souls got past the initial stage of retaining direct experience with the physical world.

As to reward and punishment, the good and bad deeds and actions of the person throughout his life, either in detail or as highlights, flashed by in less than an instant when the soul was in contact with the *"being of light"*. Nothing can be hidden from the "being". Some people interviewed characterized this as an educational effort of the indescribably loving "being" and that the "being" seemed to stress good things in life: (1) learning to love other people and (2) acquiring knowledge. In the Bahá'í Faith it is taught that the basic purpose of man is to know and to love God. When we love God, a general love for the whole of mankind becomes possible.

Clearly, as shown by Moody in *Reflections on Life After Life,* the souls had different stations, evidently depending on their actions in this physical world. Some were in "a realm of bewildered spirits", while others were free from this unfortunate condition. These confused beings seemed unable to give up their attachments to the material world. "....They seemed·bound to some particular object, person, or habit." (Moody, *Reflections on Life After Life p. 18*). They were "dulled", their consciences seemed limited compared with those of other souls not in this sad condition. They were to be in that condition only until they solved the problem or difficulty that was holding them in that state.

Now, yet another vital question arises: can belief in reincarnation be a cause for a soul to find itself in a lower station such as the "realm of bewildered spirits", after death? What if a person expects to come back to this physical world in another physical body but does-not? Could not this be a cause of confusion and bewilderment? Does belief in reincarnation, perhaps combined with other beliefs, strengthen a soul's attachment to this material world? And would this then be a cause of its finding itself in the unhappy "realm of bewildered spirits" or some other unhappy condition? The believer in reincarnation, particularly if his belief strengthens other things such as caste prejudices, lack of love and concern for others and other evils, could face an unforeseen calamitous punishment in the spiritual world. In the exalted words of the *Mahabharata:* "The divine view is this: this is the action-world and that is the fruit-world."

[*Aranya Parva, 3, 247, 35*]

Those who pass over, and are not in this confused condition, experience an indescribably wonderful, glorious state. The love the soul feels flowing from the "being of light" is inexpressible. Souls realized many truths of which they had been ignorant when they had the "vision of knowledge." In fact, after souls reached a certain point in their "near death experiences" they did not want to return to this narrow, limited, earthly world.

Dr. Moody's investigations reveal that the people who have reported "near-death experiences" often said that suicide is not the way to go to the next world. In fact, numerous people told him that they had learned that suicide was a very unfortunate act that was attended with a penalty.

[Moody, *Reflections on Life After Life, pp. 44-45*]

Of course, being a qualified psychiatrist using the tools of science, which in studies like this have limitations, Dr. Moody was cautious in drawing conclusions about his findings. He stated he was not trying to prove that there is life after death, though he personally believes in it.

As for reincarnation, Moody stated, "not one of the cases I have looked into is in any way indicative that reincarnation occurs." (Moody, *Life After Life, p. 141*). On the other hand, he states that if reincarnation does occur, an interlude in some other realm might take place between the time of separation from the old body and the entry into the new. However, he evidently was unaware that his own findings can be used to counteract this supposition. The "interlude" he refers to could be like the extraordinary, wonderful, indescribable spiritual experiences he describes from his interviewees. When they reached a certain point, especially when they contacted the "being of light", they did not want to come back. Why then would God push them back. As a punishment? In fact, some of those that returned gave the reasons why they did so—not at all for punishment but because they felt an obligation to go back and raise their children or felt they had left some important task undone or that the love or prayers of others pulled them back from death. (Moody, *Life After Life, pp. 77-81*). Also, after their return, they had lost their fear of death. They changed their attitudes, and led better lives as a result of their experiences. Would not return to this physical world after an "interlude" be a complete waste of the beneficial effects attained through existence in the spiritual world—especially when the soul was unaware of this interlude? or of what preceded it? No where do any of Dr. Moody's subjects state that they came back to this world as a punishment! Also the idea of an "interlude" may be almost as ancient as the theory of reincarnation itself, being an early attempt to defend the theory against objections to it based on the belief that the next existence is entirely spiritual. In other words, the "interlude" idea may be a compromise formulated years ago.

Thus, science, research, and reason do not consistently support the theory of reincarnation. Also, the author has found no clear cut, consistent support in the Hindu Holy Books for the theory. Many passages in the Holy Books seem against the theory, some of which are referred to in this book. When these scriptural passages are honestly translated as closely as possible to the letter and spirit of the original texts and revised in the light of all other passages as well as scientific knowledge, a contrary view can prevail. 'Abdu'l-Bahá declared, "Proofs must be asked for from the believers in reincarnation, and not conjectures, suppositions, and imaginations."

['Abdu'l-Bahá, *Some Answered Questions, p. 325*]

On this questionable basis some people have adopted beliefs, about reincarnation that knowingly or unknowingly, create many problems. Several such beliefs are investigated in the chapters that follow.

CHAPTER TWO

Believers in reincarnation say that millions (84 lakhs) physical bodies die before the soul obtains release. The soul comes back into this earthly world putting on corporeal bodies each time in order to get its reward for good deeds and to suffer the punishment of its evil deeds of past births until at last, when all sins are burned away, the soul goes on to rest permanently in the transcendental celestial world and attains to "Param-Dham" (literally: the Abode of Eternal Bliss).

Now, if every individual human soul comes into its physical birth in this world for the sake of being punished for its past life's sins and transgressions, then what about the new soul which is born in this world for the very first time? Why is fresh new soul born in this world? Has that soul also committed some sins? If so, when and where? It had no previous birth at all! If that new soul is sinless, why was it born over here?

Science tells us that life began on earth about 3,50,00,00,000 years ago. What sin did the very first creature on earth commit that determined its nature? For there was no life on earth before then. Also, according to the *Manu-Smriti* and other Hindu Scriptures, Brahman created this creation with all sorts of beings including plants, animals, humans, etc. Science tells us that life on earth at first was very simple and tiny microscopic one-celled creatures were the rule. What sins had such simple creatures committed to merit punishable lives? They could have absolutely no knowledge of what is meant by sin. What sins does a one-celled amoeba commit?

If this world, like a prison, is meant for punishing sinners, then only sinners should come here to live. They may be sinners for the first time or any millionth time. If this is the case, what right, advantage or cause is there for a brand new soul to be born in this world for the very first time?

In fact, this material earthly world is not a jail for the sinner-souls. This is the place for all new souls only and all souls created by God start in this world.

"...The spirit encircles the body at the beginning of the amalgamation of the elements and natures in the womb; the power of the spirit begins then to appear in the body gradually and successively according to the preparation and capacity to receive that everlasting abundance (of the gifts of the Lord)."

['Abdu'l-Bahá, *Tablets of 'Abdu'l-Bahá,*
Volume I, p. 157]

This divine process of creating fresh and new souls is continuous from all eternity to all eternity.

It is only during each soul's own physical lifetime on this earth that it has the liberty of conscience and voluntary action to perform either good or bad deeds on its own account and at its own risk. Good deeds will beget blessed rewards known as "Baikuntha" or "Swarga" (literally: paradise) whereas evil deeds will be punished. That punishment itself is known as "Narakagni" or hellfire. This is the divinely ordained arrangement.

Why, then, should the punishable sinners be brought back into this world? They would create unnecessary troubles for the good souls and would afflict them over here. Good souls would be tempted learn evil. There is no advantage to anyone at all.

God not punish the sinner-souls in some other world? Is He powerless to create other worlds in which this can be done? Has He got no other worlds in which this can happen? There seems to be no good reason why He cannot create a spiritual world to reward the good and punish the wicked, a world in which the good souls are protected from the mischief of the wicked.

Moreover, it is the sinning soul that is to be punished and not the body. The body was merely an instrument for the soul committing sins. That particular body is dead and gone. Why should other bodies be punished for the soul's sins committed through an old, discarded body which has absolutely nothing to do with the new body? Cannot the soul be directly punished (and rewarded) in the unmanifest soul-world? No material body is required for that purpose. To punish the soul no earthly weapon is required. No material element has any influence or-power whatsoever over the soul. Is this not indicated by the Blessed Lord in the holy *Gita* when He declared the following?

> "Weapons cannot cut it (the soul) nor can fire burn it: water cannot drench it nor can wind make it dry."
>
> *[Gita II, 23]*

In this connection the holy *Gita* clearly indicates that no being gets any manifest physical life or material body after death for either punishment or reward.

"O Bharata (Arjuna)! Beings were unmanifest in the beginning, are unmanifest in the middle, shall likewise be unmanifest on decomposition. Where comes in lamentation?"

[*Gita II, 28*]

The soul lives after death in the abstract and unmanifest soul-world assuming the unmanifest form consequent upon its actions done in this earthly life.

Through the soul's prayers, supplications, humbling itself before God, through invoking God's mercy and through the prayers and good deeds done in its name by its relatives and dear ones on this earth, its progress is hastened. The mercy of the almighty God flows to that soul in the spiritual world. In this manner, the soul's sins are eliminated or "burnt away." Ultimately the soul attains to "Mukti" or "Moksha" (liberation from imperfection). It attains the presence of God.

"From the moment the soul leaves the body and arrives in the heavenly World, its evolution is spiritual, and that evolution is: The approaching unto God."
['Abdu'l-Bahá cited in *Chalice of Immortality, p. 33*]

"When the soul attaineth the Presence of God, it will assume the form that best befitteth its immortality and is worthy of its celestial habitation."
[Bahá'u'lláh, *Gleanings from the Writings of Bahá'u'lláh, p. 157*]

In that sacred world of eternal salvation, the blessed souls will recognize and converse with each other! They will enjoy near access to the hallowed Souls of God's Manifestations, the celestial concourse of heavenly spirits, pious spirits of God's blessed saints and martyrs, and countless others who have unreservedly merged their wills into the Holy Will of God! They will relate to one another their experiences obtained in their earthly lives and experience unimaginable joy and gladness. Physical genders, lower passions, corrupt desires, greed, lust and all unholy inclinations belonging to this mundane world have no existence in that extremely blessed, most exalted, incomprehensible, unthinkable and inexpressible world. Nirvana, the Loftiest Swarga, the Eternal Moksha, the Infinite Satchitananda (literally: "the boundless joy in merging one's will into the Most Great Truth") are some terms used to this spiritual state.

These references to the spiritual world are supported by the *Swargarohana Parva* of the *Mahabharata* in the following verses:

कृतस्य कर्मणस्तत्र भुज्यते यत् फलं दिवि ।
न चान्यत् क्रियते कर्म मूलच्छेदेन भुज्यते ॥
[महाभारत, स्वर्गारोहण पर्व 3, 247, 28]

"The rewards of one's own deeds are reaped over there. No new deeds are performed. The merits of the original deeds are awarded."
[*Mahabharata, Swargarohana Parva, 3, 247, 28*]

असंतोष परितापो दृष्टा दीप्ततराः श्रियः ।
यद् भवत्यवरे स्थाने स्थितानां तत् सुदुष्करम् ॥ 30 ॥

"By beholding the splendors of the high awards being enjoyed by those who are in the loftier realms, the lower graded souls feel dissatisfied. To describe the anguish of those souls is extremely difficult."
[*Ibid. 30*]

उपरिष्टादसौ लोको योऽयं स्वरिति संज्ञितः ।
उर्ध्वगः सत्पथः शश्वद् देवयानचरो मुने ॥ 2 ॥

"O Muni! That which is called the lofty favourite
realm is much exalted. The onward movement
for attaining to that realm is elevatory, hence it is
known as the urdhvagah (up-going). That is the
right path, the excellent way. Only the divine
vehicle can carry the soul to the destination."

[*Ibid. 2*]

न वर्तयन्त्याहुतिमिस्ते नाप्यमृत भोजनाः ।
तथा दिव्य शरीरास्ते न च विग्रहमूर्तयः ॥ 21 ॥

"They do not offer oblations of sacrifices. They
do not need the nectar of immortality. Their
bodies are of divine attributes and have no particular shape."

[*Ibid. 21*]

तेजसानि शरीराणि भवन्त्यत्रोपपद्यताम् ।
कर्म जान्येव मौदगल्य न मातृ पितृ जान्यु ॥ 13 ॥

"O Moudgalya! Their bodies have glorious brilliancy which are rewards for their pious deeds.
They are not composed of mother's ovum and
father's sperm."   [*Ibid. 13*]

न संस्वदो न दौर्गन्ध्यं पुरीषं मूत्रमेव च ।
तेषां न च रजो वस्त्रं बाधते तत्र वै मुने ॥ 14 ॥

"O Muni! Those bodies never sweat nor smell
obnoxiously nor even have they any urine or
faeces. Also their clothes never become dusty."

[*Ibid. 14*]

स्वयं प्राभारते भास्वन्तो लोका: कामदुधा: परे ।
न तेषां स्त्रीकृतस्तांपो न लोकैश्वर्यमत्सर: ॥ 20 ॥

"Those of exalted realms are intrinsically illumined. They radiate light and are satisfied in
their desires. They have no lustful desires nor
ever have they any jealousy towards the
supremacy of the grandeurs of those in other
higher realms."

[*Ibid. 20*]

देवा: साध्यास्तथा विश्वे तथैव च महर्षय: ।
यामा धामाश्च मौद्गल्य गन्धर्वाप्सरसस्तथा ॥ 6 ॥
एषां देवनिकायानां प्रथक प्रथमनेकश: ।
भास्वन्त: कामसम्पन्ना लोकांस्तेजोमया: शुभा: ॥ 7 ॥

"Over there, O Moudgalya, are separate grades
of realms for the divines, for those sages who
have attained, for universal beings, for multitudes
of saints, for self-controlling restraints, for
pilgrims, for captivating heavenly choruses, for
fairies, for damsels and for many other shining
groups. All of them are the possessors of the
powers of obtaining their desired bountiful bestowals, as they are refulgent and felicitously fortunate."

[*Ibid. 6-7*]

पुरस्ताद् ब्राह्मणांस्तत्र लोकास्तेजोमया: शुभा: ।
यत्र यान्त्यृषयो ब्रह्मन् पूता स्वै: कर्मभि: शुभै: ॥ 18 ॥

"Still loftier are the realms of Brahma which are
extremely glorious and propitious where, O

Brahman, Holy Rishis with their own lustrous virtues go."

[*Ibid. 18*]

देवदूत उवाच :
ब्रह्माणः सदनादूर्ध्व तद् विष्णोः परमं पदम्।
शुद्धं सनातनं ज्योतिः परं ब्रह्मोति यद्विदुः ॥ 37 ॥

The divine Messenger said:

"Even above Brahma's realm there exists the Most Exalted Abode of the transcendental Lord Vishnu. That is the pure and eternal, most glorious station which is also called parambrahma (transcending Brahma)."

[*Ibid. 37*]

निर्ममा निरहङ्कारा निईन्द्रा संयतेन्द्रियाः ।
ध्यान योगपराश्चैव तत्र गच्छन्ति मानवाः ॥ 39 ॥

"Unselfish, having no ego, those human beings who have subdued their own sensual passion and risen up above the dual influences of pleasure and pain, and are conscientiously meditating; they are the ones who go over there."

[*Ibid. 39*]

The above mentioned holy verses of the sacred scriptures clearly depict the soul's progress and condition in the exalted spiritual world. In light of this, why should any soul have to return to this material world?

Just as a child in the womb of its mother can never understand this spacious, bright, vast and conscious world, so also, while living in this womb-like world, we cannot understand the spiritual world beyond death.

This is why in comparison with that divinely illumined spiritual world this material world is called dark by the Holy Scriptures. Terms such as द्यावा पृथिवी "Dyava prithivi" (literally: "the Illumined World") and the like are often used in the holy *Vedas*, the sacred *Gita*, and other divinely revealed scriptures.

Now let us study with unbiased minds and pure hearts what Bahá'u'lláh, the Manifestation of God for this age, has declared in His fresh Holy Revelation for the guidance of all the peoples of the world on this same subject. We will surely find the self-same eternal truths and similar statements as revealed in the Holy Scriptures of the past, including the Holy Books of the Hindus. This is because God is one, the God of the past, the present and the future. So also, religion is one, eternal in the past, eternal in the future.

"Blessed is the soul which, at the hour of its separation from the body, is sanctified from the vain imaginings of the peoples of the world. Such a soul liveth and moveth in accordance with the Will of its Creator, and entereth the all-highest paradise. The Maids of Heaven, inmates of the loftiest mansions, will circle around it, and the Prophets of God and His chosen ones will seek its companionship. With them that soul will freely converse, and will recount unto them that which it hath been made to endure in the path of God, the Lord of all worlds. The nature of the soul after death can never be described, nor is it meet and permissible to reveal its whole character to the eyes of men.... The world beyond is as different from this world as this world is different from that of the child while still in the womb of its mother. When the soul attaineth the

Presence of God, it will assume the form that best befitteth its immortality and is worthy of its celestial habitation."

[Bahá'u'lláh, *Gleanings from the Writings of Bahá'u'lláh, pp. 155-157*]

"The people of Bahá... are one and all, well aware of one another's state and condition.... They that are of the same grade and station are fully aware of one another's capacity, character, accomplishments and merits. They that are of a lower grade, however, are incapable of comprehending adequately the station, or of estimating the merits, of those that rank above them...

"The souls of the infidels, however, shall — and to this I bear witness — when breathing their last be made aware of the good things that have escaped them, and shall bemoan their plight, and shall humble themselves before God. They shall continue doing so after the separation of their souls from their bodies."

... And again :

"They that are the followers of the one true God shall, the moment they depart out of this life, experience such joy and gladness as would be impossible to describe, while they that live in error shall be seized with such fear and trembling, and shall be filled with such consternation, as nothing can exceed."

[Bahá'u'lláh, *Gleanings for the Writings of Bahá'u'lláh, pp. 169-170*]

Furthermore :

"Certain traditions of bygone ages rest on no foun-dations... Thou dost witness how most of the com-mentaries and interpretations of the words of God, now current amongst men, are devoid of truth. Their falsity hath, in some cases, been exposed when the intervening veils were rent asunder. They themselves have acknowledged their failure in ap-prehending the meaning of any of the words of God."

[Bahá'u'lláh, *Gleanings for the Writings of Bahá'u'lláh, pp. 170-171*]

As mentioned before, some believers in reincarna-tion state that the souls return to this material world to suffer punishment for the deeds of their past lives. Now, if this material world becomes a jail for punishment of the souls, of what use, then, is "Naraka" or hell. Either the souls come back on earth for punishment after death or the souls receive punishment in the spiritual hell. One or the other must take place. There is no sense in double punishment, both in the earthly and spiritual worlds. If a man drove his car once through a stop light, would the police punish him twice for it? A man should not be tried for the same crime twice. Would God be so unjust as to inflict double a punishment on souls?

If the souls return to this earthly world for punish-ment, then there is no use of any idle and unoccupied hell beyond; and if a hell does exist in the spiritual world, then it goes without saying that human souls do not return at all to this physical world. In that case, to think of a return would be a misconception.

Let us further examine the Hindu Scriptures themselves. The *Mahabharata* clearly states in its *Swargarohan Parva* that at the time when Dharmaraja Yudhisthir was ascending to paradise along with God's angels, he had to pass through hell. There he saw many sinners undergoing punishment. He asked the angels what had been the sins committed by these souls on earth for which they were suffering such severe torments.

Just pause here for a while and think carefully about that situation! Had return to the earthly world for punishment been a reality, Dharmaraja Yudhisthir would have exclaimed with surprise as to why those sinners had not been sent back to their new physical lives on earth for punishment!

Later in that same sequence the *Mahabharata* relates that Dharmaraja witnessed the sons of Dhritrashtra — The Kauravas — suffering torments of hell along with other rakshasas or devils. Then he saw his own brothers — the Pandavas — in the loftiest mansions of the Exalted Swarga, (paradise) occupying the highest thrones. He became glad when he himself entered paradise.

Now, think again minutely. Had there been reincarnation for punishment in this earthly world, why is it that the Kauravas, as well as other evil souls, were not sent back here? Why were they all kept in that spiritual world? Why were Dharmaraja Yudhisthir and all the other angels not terribly shocked by the experience of seeing the sinners in hell? Why were the sinners not sent back to the material world for punishment?

It was simply because this part of the *Mahabharata* illustrates that there is no such reincarnation as conceived by some people. The pious people of this earthly world ascend, at death, to paradise, whereas the wicked-doers fall, on death, into the spiritual hell-fire which, basically, is a condition of remoteness from God. In this connection we refer to the holy *Gita*:

हतो वा प्राप्स्यसि स्वर्गं जित्वा वा भोक्ष्यसे महीम्।
तस्मादुत्तिष्ठ कौन्तेय युद्धाय कृतनिश्चयः॥

[गीता 2: 37]

"Either slain wilt (thou) obtain paradise, or gaining victory wilt enjoy the earth; get up, therefore, O Son of Kunti (Arjuna), determined to fight."

[*Gita II, 37*]

And, how is it that Arjuna was to go unfailingly to paradise and nowhere else? This is also clarified in the holy *Gita*:

दैवी संपद्विमोक्षाय निबन्धायासुरी मता।
मा शुचः संपदं दैवीमभिजातोऽसि पाण्डव॥

[गीता 16: 5]

"The divine properties are deemed to be for liberation, the demoniacal for bondage. Grieve not, O Pandava (Arjuna), thou art born with divine properties."

[*Gita XVI, 5*]

Similarly the holy *Gita* clarifies that the wicked people go to hell after death:

अनेकचित्तविभ्रान्ता   मोहजालसमावृताः ।
प्रसक्ता कामभोगेषु पतन्ति नरकेऽशुचौ ॥

[गीता 16: 16]

"Bewildered by numerous thoughts, enmeshed in
the web of delusion, addicted to the gratification
of carnal desires, they fall into the unholy hell."
                                    [*Gita XVI, 16*]

Thus, the human soul receives chastisement for sins
and is castigated by hell-fire in the spiritual world alone
and never returns to the material world by taking birth
in any manifest physical body.

त्रिविधं नरकस्येदं   द्वारं   नाशनमात्मनः ।
कामः क्रोधस्तथा लोभस्तस्मादेवत्रयंत्यजेत् ॥

[गीता 16: 21]

"This threefold gate of hell—is destructive to the
soul; let (everyone), therefore, discard this triad."

                                    [*Gita XVI, 21*]

Does this not further support the view that as indicated in the Hindu Holy Scriptures themselves, reincarnation never takes place in this material world? Just
pause a little and again refer to the holy *Gita*:

तत्र तं बुद्धिसंयोगं   लभते पौर्वदेहिकम् ।
यतते च ततो भूयः संसिद्धौ कुरुनन्दन ॥

[गीता 6: 43]

"Over there that (soul) realizes intellectual consciousness of the previous body and thereupon

redoubles its efforts for the perfect attainment, O
Rejoice of the Kurus (Arjuna)."

[*Gita VI, 43*]

The word "tatra" means "over there" or "in that
world," not "over here" or "in this world."

Moreover, the soul burdened with evil deeds, in ad-
dition to its having knowledge of that spiritual world
wherein it then lives after physical death also retains a
consciousness of the total life it led in the physical body.
According to the *Gita* (*VI, 43*) just referred to, it is this
that constructively helps it to redouble its efforts in
order to attain the perfect bliss. Its efforts over there will
be of the nature of repentance, humbling itself, begging
for the mercy of God, as no new and independent deeds
can be performed over there like those that were performed in the physical world.

Some Hindus believe that the spirits or souls of their
beloved and respected forefathers help protect and/or
guard them. For example, a farmer believes that the soul
of his dead grandfather protects his family's fields. But if
their forefathers had taken other births such as plants or
more divergent forms, how are those souls free to come
and help these people?

In the *Ramayana* which is very popular with the
Hindu masses, we clearly see that King Dashrath appears from Swarga (paradise) to his son Rama who was
in Lanka, 14 years after his father's death, and blesses
him. Not only this, but, at the request of his son, Dashrath forgives Kaikeyee, Rama's step-mother, who had
been the cause of all their sufferings and because of
whom Rama, Sita and Laxman were exiled for 14 years.

This means that, as perceived by the writer of the *Ramayana*, King Dashrath was not sent by God to this world for enjoying the sweet fruits of his good deeds nor for suffering punishment for his errors.

Hindus generally have a 30 day month (Shradh) every year in which they feed Brahmins, their own families, and poor people in memory of their forefathers and for the benefit and progress of their souls. They say prayers, read Holy Books and carry out charitable work in the name of their forefathers. If their forefathers had already taken rebirth (or perhaps many such rebirths) in this world in other forms such as plants, animals, or other human beings unrelated to them in another society, what good would all these efforts be during this month?

Most Hindus believe that the marriage between a husband and wife is a strong bond between the two souls. When the husband dies, the widow doesn't remarry. They say that for a woman the husband is like God (pati parmeshwar). Their bond is eternal. Even after her husband's death, she is still married to her husband's soul. Why should she marry someone else? But if her husband has taken another birth (or many births) in another form, such as a woman or another man or animal or plant, what kind of relationship does the widow have with her husband's soul? Then, when she dies, if she also is supposed to be reborn as another human being and her husband has also been reborn and both of them marry other people; what sort of relationship would they have then? How can they retain their eternal bond? Instead, they are in a mess! On the other hand, an eternal bond is only possible when they both go to the spiritual realm and live there together lovingly making progress to attain nearness to God.

Thus, when we compare the beliefs of Hindus on reincarnation with other beliefs they hold, we run into all sorts of contradictions and confusion. Let us investigate yet another of these suppositions. People say that some children are born with physical and mental defects, poor, destitute, with criminal tendencies, in low castes or as untouchables, etc... as a punishment for the deeds of their past lives.

Why are children born physically or mentally defective? In this age of science we are well aware of the causes of such defects. Mistakes of the pregnant mother can permanently harm the child in the womb. Venereal and chronic constitutional diseases of one or both the parents in the form of latent miasma are inherited by the children.

Children during their mothers' pregnancies are directly and/or indirectly affected by many influences (samskaras—literally: impressions or impacts on the mind and the body) including social and economic conditions such as wealth or poverty, diet, fear, shock, accidents, devotion or lack of devotion to God, religious beliefs, superstitions and blind beliefs, dreams, the company of friends, and individual and collective actions such as taking drugs, drinking alcohol, smoking, and innumerable other factors—not by the deeds of an assumed past life.

Science has proved that the mother's diet during pregnancy may cause various diseases like cretinism mental retardation, drug addiction, growth retardation, a missing or an extra limb and even a weak or sickly disposition. Various genetic diseases may cause the newly born child to be defective in health, limbs or intellect. Examples of this are, Mongolism, cancers, some heart and skin diseases.

This is supported by the ancient Hindu system of medicine, the Ayurveda, in Shushrut Samhita, Shavir Sthan — Shushrut Adhyay.

Just as the pregnant mother's wrong diet creates diseases in the child, similarly harmful food or bad habits spoil the sperm of the father — in this manner whichever child is conceived may be physical defects.

It has also been proved by medical science that the foetus in the mother's womb can be affected by the mothers emotional state and environment as also by the company she keeps.

These foregoing scientific proofs establish the fact that the physical or mental defects of the child are due to genetic causes or the wrong feeding, the unhygenic and undesirable environment in which the father and mother live at the time of conception of the child and the pregnancy period.

In this connection the *Manu-Smriti* declares:

यत्र नार्यस्तु पूज्यन्ते रमन्ते तत्र देवताः ॥

[मनुस्मृति 3, 56]

"Where the woman is adored play the brilliant ones."

[*Manu Smriti, 3, 56*]

Note that, according to the ancient medical knowledge (Ayurveda) no mention is made whatsoever that these defects are due to the actions of a previous life! Modern medicine too supports this.

Scientists and medical experts are working to find the causes of defects in early childhood and indeed throughout life so that much of this can be prevented and treated. As this occurs and there will be less defects and suffering among the people. Yet moral behaviour continues to deteriorate. Does this mean that there is less punishment for deeds in the life? No, it is due to the advancement of science and medicine.

We use scientific knowledge, not suppositions and conjectures, to understand why children suffer from physical and mental defects in life, both before and after birth. As referred to previously, in the words of the blessed Lord in the *Gita*:

"He who is well contented with knowledge and science is called a yogi, the conqueror of senses, who stands steadfast as if on a rock."

[Gita VI, 8]

"To thee, the uncarping, verily shall I declare this most profound secret: having knowledge through common sense along with science (systematized knowledge), thou shalt have salvation, freed from misfortune."

[Gita IX, 1]

Belief must be tested by science and common sense as well as reference to the Holy Scriptures; otherwise it may become an impediment to understanding reality.

In the Vedas and in other Scriptures, medical science teaches us how to cure people and prolong life. Countless herbs and chemicals are also given by God. This shows that our lives in this world are precious and for preservation and not for punishment at the hands of other persons — who may also be sinners in one way or another.

Some Hindus believe that incapacitating accidents occur to people as punishments for deeds performed in past lives. In this connection, as mentioned previously, it is proclaimed by God through Shri Krishna in the *Gita, II, 13*:

Just as the dweller in the body has childhood, youth, (and) old age, following the same way (soul) gets a different body; the wise does not get deluded thereby.

Thus childhood is the past life (purwa-janma) of the present young man who will, in turn, gradually be further born at a later stage in the old-age body, which will be his next life (punar-janma).

If a soul neglects its education in its child-body, it suffers the ill consequences in its subsequent bodies: the youth-body and the old-age body. If a naughty child plays mischief and fall breaking his hand or leg or blinding his eyes, he remains incapacitated, lame or blind in his subsequent births viz. into the youth-body and thereafter the old-age-body until he casts off this senile old-age-body which is his final body on earth. Therefore the soul suffers the consequences of actions that took place in the child's life and not the consequences from a supposed life before conception in the mother's womb.

After birth, children are punished and rewarded by parents and teachers so that they may improve their character. Sound principles of child psychology and pedagogy should be followed. If a child is punished for his actions by his educator, he must understand why he is being punished. This will aid in preventing the repetition of the misbehaviour. If a judge punishes a condemned criminal for his crime, the culprit must know why he is being punished. There is absolutely no sense in punishing a man for an undeclared crime. If he does not know the sins for which he is apparently being punished, he can keep on committing the same sins. No improvement in his character takes place. The punishment must be specifically connected to the misbehaviour or crime, otherwise the punishment is dangerously unjust. The person punished will feel this injustice deeply and may even rebel against punishment itself. Isn't God, the Knower of all things, capable of a better approach to reward and punishment? Yet followers of the theory of reincarnation persist in the belief that children (and adults) are punished by being born physically or mentally defective, incapacitated, poor, destitute, in low castes or as untouchables, etc... due to unknown actions in a supposed past life! Such punishment does not arouse sincere repentance. How then can any improvement take place at all?

Some Hindus believe that human beings may be reborn as animals, fish, birds, serpents, insects, trees and plants or stones or some other inanimate objects. We definitely know through science that unlike human neither the things in the mineral kingdom nor vegetables and not even animals have abstract intelligence. Hence, how can minerals, plants, or animals understand about being punished for past sins or rewarded with goodly gifts and divine bounties during their life spans? How can any mineral, plant or animal improve to be a human again under these circumstances? Moreover, if a mineral or plant or animal was once a human, why doesn't the mineral, plant or animal have human intelligence? Without human intelligence, how can it appreciate rewards or repent after punishments? What, then, is the sense of rewards or punishment?

Believers in reincarnation often link this with belief in predestiny. People are often heard to say something like: "O God! What sins have we committed for which Thou art punishing us in this way?" When in trouble or misfortune, they connect this misfortune with the unknown evil deeds of a supposed previous life and, as a result, do not investigate the true causes of the problems. Further, people come to them to console them by saying that this calamity must have been predestined by God. But in this connection, the *Yogavashishtha* says:

दैवेन त्वभियुक्तोऽअं तत्करोमदृशं स्थितम् ।
समाश्वासनवागेषा न दैवं परमार्थतः ॥

[योग वशिष्ठ 2: 8:15]

"Predestiny is merely a consolation for persons of lower intellectual level at the time of calamities and griefs. Otherwise, in reality, there is nothing like divine predestiny for everyone."

[*Yogavashishtha II, 8:15*]

In the *Gita* also the Blessed Lord has said a similar thing:

न कर्तृत्वं न कर्माणि लोकस्य सृजति प्रभुः ।
न   कर्मफलसंयोगं   स्वभावस्तु   प्रवर्तते ॥

[गीता 5: 14]

"The Lord determines neither the doership nor
the doings of beings nor even their contant with
the fruits of actions. It is nature that functions."

[*Gita V, 14*]

Many believers in reincarnation also believe that
Brahmans; the priests, Kshatriyas; the warriors and
kings, Vaishyas: the merchants, and Shudras: the ser-
vants are the four castes of human beings created by
God Himself. When anyone is born in any of these castes, he or she is reaping the fruits of his own deeds,
good or bad, of his past lives. This is how the so-called
higher caste people have been taking benefits of even
the meanest and the most inhuman kinds of services,
from shudras, the people of low caste, and yet hatefully
calling them Asprushyas, the Untouchables. Yet, among
the first, second and third highest castes human unity is
lacking and the dignity of each person is not preserved.
Even among the members of each caste there have
arisen innumerable subcastes and petty-sub-castes, with
deep down feelings of alienation against each other.
This is largely due to the fact that people are commonly
inclined to think that all others are the product of the
deeds of their past lives, and none may pity anyone else
except himself. Natural human feelings of loving compassion, mercy, and forgiveness are suppressed by feelings that arise from the theory of the just ice of rebirth
linked to the belief in reincarnation. Nor, do we see a
higher spiritual capacity in all individuals of higher cas-

tes as we would expect if the belief in rebirth was actually valid.

Today, the world is rapidly changing, society is changing, the caste system is breaking down. The old caste groups, which were of some use for carrying out duties and functions of a bygone era, have now become rigid and oppressive. The progressive mentality of some people and the laws of the country are helping to gradually change the old beliefs of orthodox followers so that the so-called low caste people are no longer tyranised as they used to be.

The religious law also changes with time. There are basically two types of teachings in religion: firstly, those that are eternal and fundamental, such as the Law of Love, and, secondly, those social ordinances that are not eternal but change as centuries pass and societies evolve. These include ordinances concerning health, diet, marriage, etc... Lord Krishna's teaching in the *Gita* about the four social groups, the Brahmans, Kshatriyas, Vaishyas, and Shudras, was never meant to be eternal, rigid, and fixed as some Hindus regard it. If God intended it to be eternal and everlasting, why would the caste system be breaking down and disintegrating today?

Thus, the following passage in the *Gita* should not be regarded as creating four water-tight compartments of four different groups of people:

ब्राह्मणक्षत्रियविशां शूद्राणां च परंतप ।
कर्माणि प्रविभक्तानि स्वभावप्रभवैर्गुणैः ॥

[गीता 18: 41]

"The work of Brahmans, Kshatriyas, Vaishyas and Shudras, O Conqueror of Foes (Arjuna), is separated as per everyone's nature-oriented qualities."

[*Gita XVIII, 41*]

Let us now see what were the duties and functions prescribed in the *Gita* for persons in each of these four social groups:

शमो दमस्तपः शौचं क्षान्तिरार्जवमेव च ।
ज्ञानं विज्ञानमास्तिक्यं ब्रह्मकर्म स्वभावजम् ॥

[गीता 18: 42]

"Serenity, self-restraint, austerity, purity, forgiveness, uprightness, and even knowledge, science and belief in God are the nature-born deeds of Brahmans."

[*Gita XVIII, 42*]

शौर्यं तेजो धृतिर्दाक्ष्यं युद्धे चाप्यपलायनम् ।
दानमीश्वर भावश्च क्षात्रं कर्म स्वभावजम् ॥

[गीता 18: 43]

"Bravery, splendour, steadfastness, dexterity in battle, as also not to flee away cowardly, generosity, charity and lordliness are the nature-born deeds of Kshatriyas."

[*Gita XVIII, 43*]

कृषिगौरक्ष्यवाणिज्यं वैश्यकर्म स्वभावजम् ।
परिचर्यात्मकं कर्म शूद्रस्यापि स्वभावजम् ॥

[गीता 18: 44]

"Agriculture, cattle caring and trade, the nature-born duties of the Vaishyas. The duty of Shudras is attending to the service, that also is born of nature."

[*Gita XVIII, 44*]

यतः प्रवत्तिभूतानां येन सर्वमिदं ततम्।
स्वकर्मणा तमभ्यर्च्य सिद्धिं विन्दति मानवः ॥

[गीता 18: 46]

"He from whom all beings are activated, by Whom all this pervaded, worshiping Him through one's own dutiful deeds, man achieves accomplishment."

[*Gita XVIII, 46*]

In none of these passages is there any reference to Purvajanma (previous birth) or the deeds of past lives and their rewards or punishments to be borne by human beings in these four classifications.

As we noted above, love is an eternal teaching of religion. No changes and chances of the ages and nations and no revolutions of conditions, howsoever drastic they may happen to be, can alter the ever-advancing, universal, eternal Law of Love.

According to the Law of Love, God loves His creation; we the creatures should therefore also love God and at the same time love one another. We should love all other human beings with a spark of the love of God. This is what has been taught to us right from the time of the *Rigveda* the most ancient known and still extant command of God on earth:

संड्ड्च्छध्वं सं वदध्वं सं वो मनांसि जानताम् ।
देवाभागं   यथा पूर्वे   सञ्जानाना   उपासते ॥
समानोमन्त्र समितिः समानी समानंमनः सहचित्तेमेषाम् ।
समानं मन्त्रमभि मन्त्रये वः समानेन वो हविषाजुहोमि ॥

समानी व आकूतिः समाना हृदयानि वः ।
समानमस्तुः वो मनोयथा वः सुसहासति ॥

[ऋग्वेद खण्ड 7, अष्टक 8, मन्डल 10, अं. 8,
व 49/3; अं. सूत्र 191/मंत्र संख्या 2, 3 तथा 4]

"Like the enlightened ones of the past who used
to acquire their share in unity, live ye all in harmony with one another, consort in loving sweetness with all, be one in thought and in knowledge.

Let mind-protecting Divine Commandment be
equal to all, let there be equal commingling of ye
all, let all your minds be as one mind, and all your
attentions be in accord. I command ye all to be
equal under One Holy Command, I bring ye up
all alike offering Myself as a sacrifice.

Be united in your purpose, let your hearts be as
one heart, and your minds be as one mind,
so that your affairs may be co-operatively well
organized."

[*Rig Veda Khand 7, Ashtak VIII, Mandal 10,
8-49/3/3, 10-191, verses 2-4*]

Do these blessed words from the *Rig Veda* support
the caste system in any way. Do they not instal in our
hearts and minds the conviction that the disunity, dishar-
mony, hatred, inequality, and opposition inherent in the
caste system must be replaced with unity, harmony,

loving sweetness, equal commingling, oneness of mind and heart, and cooperatively well organized affairs.

This principle of unity is repeated over and over again in the world's great religions. Bahá'u'lláh, the Manifestation of God for this modern age, has made it the cornerstone of His teachings. The greatest need for mankind today is universal love and unity, not the preservation and perpetuation of caste, racism, etc...

Bahá'u'lláh declared:

"The utterance of God is a lamp, whose light is these words: Ye are the fruits of one tree, and the leaves of one branch. Deal ye one with another with the utmost love and harmony, with friendliness and fellowship. He Who is the light of unity that it can illuminate the whole earth. The One true God, He Who knoweth all things, Himself testifieth to the truth of these words."

[Bahá'u'lláh, *Writings of Bahá'u'lláh, pp. 310-311*]

Believers in reincarnation quote certain passages from Hindu Holy Scriptures an attempt to support the theory. The author has already cited some of them. Persons using the following verse from the *Gita* often avoid the first three words so that it looks like this:

"...Death is certain of that which is born; birth is certain of that which is dead. You should not therefore lament over the inevitable."

[*Gita II, 27*]

But this is not the simple, straightforward divine verdict in the *Gita*. The person should, instead, add the three words, ponder on the whole verse and the previous one, and see the connection between the two.

अथ चैनं नित्यजातं नित्यं वा मन्यसे मृतम् ।
तथापि त्वं महाबाहो नैवं शोचितुमर्हसि ॥
जातस्य हि ध्रुवो मृत्युर्ध्रुवं जन्म मृतस्य च ।
तस्मादपरिहार्येऽर्थे न त्वं शोचितुमर्हसि ॥

[गीता 2: 26]

"And, O Mighty-armed (Arjuna), even if you regard this (soul) as constantly taking birth and constantly dying, you should not grieve like this.

In that case death is certain of that which is born; birth is certain of that which is dead. You should not therefore lament over the inevitable."

[*Gita II, 26-27*]

In verse 26 the Blessed Lord has stated to Arjuna, "... even if you regard this (soul) as constantly taking birth..." Thus the Blessed Lord was questioning Arjuna's thinking about death and rebirth, even if the words introduce the element of uncertainty and negation. The Blessed Lord did not say "... this (soul) is constantly taking birth and constantly dying, so you should not grieve like this." In other words, there is no support at all for the theory of reincarnation in these verses.

Also, with regard to the words in verse 27, "... birth is certain of that which is dead...", we have already referred to a verse in the *Aitariya Upanishada* that states that death here and entrance into the next world is termed a third birth. In this connection the findings of Dr. Moody and many others into near-death experiences can be understood to show that the soul's release from the body into the spiritual world may very well be like a "birth", as it is such an unexpectedly new, different, sudden experience — just as the child experiences at the time of its birth into this physical world.

CHAPTER THREE

God, in His own inscrutable wisdom, and as a token of His supreme favor, has through His boundless love and infinite mercy, made a very special arrangement to guide mankind. He sends a divine Manifestation, Who appears as a human being, at certain intervals when God Himself deems it to be fit and necessary. This He has regularly announced in the Holy Scriptures of the world. We find in the *Srimad Bhagwad Gita:*

यदा यदा हि धर्मस्य ग्लानिर्भवति भारत।
अभ्युत्थानमधर्मस्य तदाऽऽत्मानं सृजाम्यहम्॥
परित्राणाय साधूनां विनाशाय च दुष्कृताम्।
धर्मसंस्थापनार्थाय सम्भवामि युगे युगे॥

[गीता 4, 7-8]

The Mighty Lord said:

"Whensoever there occurs a decline of religion, O Bharat (Arjuna), and the rise of irreligion, it is then that I send forth My Spirit. For the full protection of those who attain (to that spirit), for the destruction in a particular manner (in every age) of the wicked-doers, and to institutionalise religion, make I Myself (manifest) possible from age to age."

[*Gita IV, 7-8*]

This same truth is expressed in the *Ram-Charit Manas* in these words:

जब जब होई धरम कै हानि,
बाढ़हि असुर, अधम, अभिमानी।

तब तब प्रभु धरि विविध सरीरा।
हरहिं कृपानिधि सज्जन पीरा॥
असुर मारि थापहि सुरन्ह राखहि निज स्रुति-सेतु।
जग विस्तारहि विसद जस राम-जनम कर हेतु॥

[तुलसी कृत रामचरित मानस, बाल काण्ड,
प्रथम सोपान, 129]

"From time to time whenever religion is decreased and the unholy, the irreligious, and the haughty people increase, the Lord takes a body, different from time to time, and removeth, through His infinite bounties, the calamities of the good people. He destroyeth the unholy, establisheth holiness and protecteth the chain (bridge) of His own sacred knowledge and diffuseth His Immaculate Glory in the world. The same is the motive of His Holiness Rama's birth."

[Tulsi, *Ramcharit Manas, Bal Kand,*
1st Sopan, 129]

The holy Vedas also say the same thing in these words:

अहं रुद्राय धनुरातनोमि ब्रह्मद्विषे शरखे हंतवा ज।
अहं जनाय समदं कृणोम्यहं द्यावावृथिनि आ विवेश॥

[अथर्ववेद 4, 30-5]

"I stretch bow for the oppressed in order to kill the tyrant and also the enemies of God; I create all happiness for the people, I enter, prevailed in heaven and earth, clad in the attire of Manifestation."

[*Atharva Veda, IV, 30-5*]

वेदाहमेतं पुरुषं महान्तमादित्य वर्णं तमसः जरस्तात् ।
तमेव विदित्वाति मृत्युमेति नान्यः पंथा विद्यतेऽयनाय ॥
प्रजापतिश्चर:ति गर्भेऽन्तरजायमानो बहुधा विजायते ।
तस्य योनि परिपश्यन्ति धीरास्तस्मिन्ह तुस्थुर्भवनानि विश्वा ॥

[यजुर्वेद 31: 18-19]

"I know that Most Great Ruler Who, like the brilliancy of the sun, is beyond darkness; having known Him alone is crossed the mortal stage; no way is known for going but this.

The Essentially Unmanifestable moveth within, the Lord of generations vividly manifesting Himself repeatedly; the steadfast behold from all sides the Abode of the Original Cause; in that abide the worlds of the universe."

[*Yajur Veda, XXXI, 18-19*]

The Manifestation of God is the Meeting Point between God and man on earth. *Shrimad Bhagwad Gita* describes the Manifestation of the Divine Being on earth in these holy words:

अवजानन्ति मां मूढा मानुषीं तनुमाश्रितम् ।
परं भावमजानन्तो मम भूतमहेश्वरम् ॥

[गीता 9: 11]

"The foolish disobey Me when I am clad in a human body; they know not My transcendental nature; I am the Great Lord of beings."

[*Gita IX, 11*]

Not only in the Hindu Scriptures but also in other religious Holy Books this same thing has been described. The *Qur'án* says: "O the misery of men! No

Messenger cometh unto them but they laugh Him to scorn" *(Qur'án 36: 30)*. Again He saith: "Each nation has plotted darkly against their Messenger to lay violent hold on Him, and disputed with vain words to invalidate the truth."

[*Qur'án 40: 5*]

Bahá'u'lláh in this connection further explains:

"Verily He who is the Day-star of Truth and Revealer of the Supreme Being holdeth, for all time, undisputed sovereignty over all that is in heaven and on earth, though no man be found on earth to obey Him. He verily is independent of all earthly dominion, though He be utterly destitute. Thus We reveal unto thee the mysteries of the Cause of God, and bestow upon thee the gems of divine wisdom, that haply thou mayest soar on the wings of renunciation to those heights that are veiled from the eyes of men.

[Bahá'u'lláh, *Writings of Bahá'u'lláh, p. 97*]

"It is clear and evident to thee that all the Prophets (Manifestations of God) are the Temples of the Cause of God, Who have appeared clothed in diverse attire. If thou wilt observe with discriminating eyes, thou wilt behold them all abiding in the same tabernacle, soaring in the same heaven, seated upon the same throne, uttering the same speech, and proclaiming the same Faith. Such is the unity of those Essences of being, those Luminaries of infinite and immeasurable splendour. Wherefore, should one of these Manifestations of Holiness proclaim saying: "I am the return

of all the Prophets," He verily speaketh the truth. In like manner, in every subsequent Revelation, the return of the former Revelation is a fact, the truth of which is firmly established. Inasmuch as the return of the Prophets of God, as attested by verses and traditions, hath been conclusively demonstrated, the return of their chosen ones also is therefore definitely proven. This return is too manifest in itself to require any evidence or proof.
[Bahá'u'lláh, *Kitáb-i-íqán, pp. 97-98*]

The purpose of the Manifestation of God appearing in this world age after age is thus described in the holy *Gita*:

यद्यदाचरति श्रेष्ठस्तत्तदेवेतरो जनः ।
स यत्प्रमाणं कुरुते लोकस्तदनुवर्तते ॥
नमे पार्थास्ति कर्तव्यं त्रिषु लोकेषुर्किंचन ।
नानवाप्तमवाप्तव्यं वर्त स्व च कर्मति ॥
यदि ह्हं न वर्तेयं जातु कर्मण्यतन्द्रितः ।
मम वर्त्यानुवर्तन्ते मनुष्याः पार्थ सर्वशः ॥
उत्सीदेयुरिमे लोका न कुर्यां कर्म चेदहम् ।
संकरस्य च कर्ता स्यामुपहन्याभिमाः प्रजाः ॥
[गीता 3: 21-24]

"Whatsoever the Most Great Man doeth, the other people also do. It is He who setteth forth the standard, by that the people go.

Neither the least work is there in the three worlds, O Partha (literally: the Son of earth) (Arjuna) which should be done by Me, nor is there any unobtained thing which should be obtained; still I occupy Myself in action.

Should I not always occupy Myself, the un-
wearied, in action, the people all around, O Partha, would follow My Path.

Were I not to perform action, these people would
be destroyed; and, in that case, I would slay these
generations."

[*Gita III, 21-24*]

God allows every human soul the liberty to think and
act according to its own inherent capacity to decide between the good and the bad. Each soul selects a course
of action by his/her own free choice — right or wrong.
The Lord gives these lessons, age after age, to keep souls
on the straight path of adopting divine virtues in life.
God does this by repeatedly sending forth His Holy
Manifestation (the Avatar) on earth in a human form.
The Avatar gives pious advice in words and also
demonstrates by His own example how to live in a saint-
ly manner in this world. This is nothing but a divine
method of guiding the people aright. This is characteristic of revealed religion.

Thus, in every age, there is a new revelation of God's
new lessons for human beings exactly in accordance with
the progress of human society both mental as well as
spiritual. The most fundamental lesson God teaches
each human being is the lesson of love. Love for God
and love for all other human beings. To teach this essence of religion, the Manifestation of God, in His
authority as the sole mouthpiece of God, commands us
to love one another for the sake of the love of God. In
His capacity as a simple human being, the Avatar actually loves us and practically demonstrates the meaning of
love in action. While loving us He is confronted with

bitter opposition and surrounded by severe afflictions and torture which He patiently bears. He thus teaches us a lesson in patience and forbearance.

For example, His Holiness Jesus Christ was a Manifestation of God on earth. His opponents determined to put Him to death. The evening before He was to be crucified, He went into the garden of Gethsemane and sincerely prayed to God saying: "Father, all things are possible for you. Take this cup away from Me; nevertheless, not what I will, but what You will." (Mark 14: 36). We know that this prayer of Lord Jesus was not granted by God, and Lord Jesus' body had to be crucified. In spite of that supreme affliction and unbearable test, Lord Jesus remained not only steadfast but also, at the last moment of His earthly life, prayed to God to forgive those who were crucifying Him because they knew not what they were doing.

This teaches, all of us, for all times to come, to live virtuous lives and to remain steadfast until our physical death. We should sincerely and lovingly forgive even those who inflict woes and tyrannies upon us. Each human being can do it if he but chooses to think in the right way and to do the right thing. A Manifestation of God, while performing human duties in His earthly life, takes help from the Divine Source. Any other human being can also follow this path. However he first has to decide to do it and seek help from God. He should not be disappointed even if the help, as wished or hoped for, is not forthcoming at once. Such are the martyrs in the path of God's religion in every age. Thus the followers of a religion, like the followers of previous religions before them can be so transformed that they would renounce for the sake of God their families, their beliefs, and even their lives. These souls reap the rewards of their pious actions in the spiritual world and can reach the presence of God.

In this way each religion is the resurrection of its predecessor religion. Similar circumstances, more or less, appear each time. This is the renewal of religion, and the return of the Manifestation of God. This is the repetition of history in which many things reappear, including similar personalities, similar clashes of thought, similar tyrants, similar victims, especially among the followers of religion, and similar opposition, tests, and calamities as well as similar victories. In sum, from this point of view, religion is renewed, the Manifestations return, and their followers return. Thus the familiar expression, "History repeats itself."

In the light of the foregoing discussion we can now investigate the underlying meaning and significance of the following holy verses of the *Shrimad Bhagwad Gita*:

श्री भगवान उवाच:
बहूनि मे व्यतीतानि जन्मानि तव चार्जुन।
तान्यहं वेद सर्वाणि न त्वं तेत्थ परंतप॥
अजोऽपि सन्नव्ययात्मां भूतानामीश्वरोऽपि सन्।
प्रकृति स्वामधिष्ठाय सम्भवाम्यात्ममायया॥

[गीता 4: 5-6]

The Mighty Lord Speak:

"Many births of Mine have passed, and thine, O Arjun; all these do I know, but thou knowest not. O chastiser of foes (Arjuna).

Though being the Unborn, as well as essentially
the Inexhaustible Self, as also the Lord of all
beings, I make Myself Manifest by subduing My
own nature through My innate (Divine) Apparition (Maya)."

[*Gita IV, 5-6*]

Thus, this divine proclamation of Shri Krishna in the
Gita refers to the return of the Manifestation. The Holy
Spirit that comes to the Manifestation is one, but They
are different physical men. Similarly devoted followers
such as Arjuna are found in every religion; they are different physical men and women. This passage should be
understood at a deeper level rather than just interpret-
ing it to establish the concept of reincarnation which we
have found from our discussion so far, is a fallacy. The
Bahá'í writings accept the concept of the return of attributes, so it is true in a sense, that persons like Arjuna
are born in every age.

In these verses there is a specific mention of God's
own Maya, His Innate Divine Apparition. This is an extraordinary power of divinity alone with which the ordi-
nary physical birth and death of human beings should
not be confused. The Blessed Lord cannot be born or
make Himself die. He transcends both birth and death.
He is the Lord of all beings. His birth refers to the coming of God's Manifestation on earth to fulfil a specific
purpose as given in the *Gita IV, 7-8*. God's manifestation
on earth is also referred to in the *Yajur Veda XXXI, 19*
and in the *Gita IX, 11* mentioned previously.

Usually people translate the word "Maya" as "illusion." The religion of God is not "illusion", nor are
divine religious matters "illusive." God's sending forth

of His Holy Spirit into this world from age to age is not an illusion. God does not create illusions' but reality. He wants to clear all illusions from the insight of each and every human being.

Religion is a divine substantial fact. It is the most important of all that is important to man in this world. It is for this that God reveals His divine religion age after age through His Manifestations Who become "apparent" to the human world in the bodies of human beings. God is the Most Invisible of the invisible. He is the transcendental Spirit, incomprehensible to anyone else except Himself. So in every age He sands forth His Most Great Representative – through Whose pure soul He reveals Himself. Through Him He contacts the human world. He lives in it. He is the authentic Mouthpiece of God, – releasing the newly revealed Word of God, He talks with human beings. He loves them: He opens wide their spiritual eyes. He gives them new higher bestowals and lessons. He solves their problems, by helping them at every step in life. He elevates their souls to greater heights than in a previous age. He changes their circumstances by establishing a new order; giving them newer and broader institutions to facilitate their day-to-day functioning. He teaches the newest methods and techniques: raising their physical, mental, psychological, spiritual, educational, economic, social, and political states and all other levels of their lives, both outwardly as well as inwardly. In other words, each Manifestation of God inspires a new era of human power. He releases a fresh measure of divine Grace and renews man's energy.

Such is the dawn of a divine day for human beings on earth. The Author of this is the Holy Manifestation of

God—a Messenger of the Divine Being, a Mouthpiece of God Himself, an Ishwari Avatar, a Divine Rishi, a Major Prophet of God, a Rasul from Alláh, an Asho Vakhshur, a Divinely Enlightened Tathagata—the Holy Person Who possessed the Boddhi Satta, the Apparitor of the Divine King of Kings. Saint Charan Das, in one of his heart-enchanting couplets, expounds this very truth in simple words, short and sure:

निराकार सो   ब्रह्म है   माया है   आकार।
दोनों पदवी को लिये ऐसा पुरुष निहार॥

[संत चरणदास]

"The Brahma is formless, Maya has forms;
Behold a Personage wieldeth both the norms!"

[Saint Charan Das]

Thus a new religious dispensation of the Cause of God appears. A typical pattern is followed each time. In the beginning very few persons believe and accept this new and broader dimension of truth. The majority rejects it and tyrants torment the believers. But gradually the tide is turned and the new Faith of God prevails far and wide and better conditions become apparent. The religion reaches a peak and is associated with a great civilization. But then the religion weakens, hatred and disunity replace love and harmony, and a new religious cycle begins with the appearance of a new religion from God. The seed of the old, dying tree is planted and a new, young tree grows and flourishes.

Such similar cycles come repeatedly, each one being superseded by the next. This is called the birth and re-birth of religion. God's Manifestations, Their followers and Their opponents are all reborn, in this way.

Now a new light shines upon the verses from the *Gita:* it illuminates our understanding of the births and lives of the Manifestations of God through Maya. Shri Krishna's own manifestation in this world five thousand years ago is an example.

Although the Mighty Lord is invisible and unattainable and human beings cannot understand His essence, He still guides mankind through His Holy Spirit which He sends forth in every age. His Manifestation then appears in the form of a human personage and in a specific way religion is once again established and peace and prosperity become possible for mankind. There is no physical birth involved.

जन्म कर्म च मे दिव्यमेवं यो वेत्ति तत्त्वत: ।
त्यक्त्वा देहं पुनर्जन्म नैति मामेति सोऽर्जुन ॥

[गीता 4: 9]

"He who knoweth in essence My divine birth and action, having abandoned the body, is not born again; cometh he unto Me, O Arjun!"

[*Gita IV, 9*]

After physical death the human soul makes an entry into the realm of the spirits, which is a spiritual birth over there in the Paraloka. The foregoing verse indicates that in the spiritual worlds beyond, the sanctified soul will not have to take birth again and again in its journey to God. The Bahá'í Writings indicate 'rebirth' in the spiritual world after our passing away from the earth. There are endless Spiritual worlds of God. The human soul can either journey through each one of them or attain the presence of God without having to do so. However, there is no rebirth for the human soul in the

material world again. Then the final attainment of that
soul, according to the Darshan Shastra, the science of
attaining to the highest station of seeing God (literally:
Darshan), is to come to the presence of God. There is no
higher station for a soul than this according to any
philosophy in the world; the Hindu belief is no excep-
tion. We, like the devoted followers of the religions of
the past, can in this modern age follow the same spiritual
path toward the presence of God.

Let us read from the holy *Gita* the verse immediately
following:

वीतरागभयक्रोधा   मन्मया   मामुपाश्रिताः ।
बहवो   ज्ञानतपसा   पूता   मद्भावमागताः ॥

[गीता 4: 10]

"Freed from attachment, fear and anger, mentally absorbed in Me, taking refuge in Me, purified
by the fire of knowledge, many have attained
unto My nature."

[Gita IV, 10]

Here there is a specific mention of the higher
spiritual nature. In physical nature there is selfishness,
attachment to this mundane world, lack of faith in God,
anger, hatred. But the divine nature is quite different. It
is characterized by the divine virtues of generosity, forgiveness, tolerance, obliging others without selfish mo-
tives, trust in God, and pious actions and deeds all
dedicated to the love of God. No reward is anticipated.
This is called by Shri Krishna "Nishkam Karma" (unselfish deeds). So, God assures us that those who subdue
their own lower nature and rise up to the higher spiritual

nature will attain unto His nature. Again, we can be like the devoted followers of the past religions and develop our spiritual nature.

In this connection, we have to remember that "Punarjanma" as stated in the Holy Books is a series of birth after birth, and not birth after death and then again birth and again death, and so on. In the *Aiteriya Upanishada* we have seen that there are three births of a human being: at conception, at the delivery of the child, and when the body dies. Then the soul enters the world of the spirits. The holy *Gita* says the "soul-body" is neither cut by weapons, nor burnt by fire, nor drenched by water, nor dried by wind. This is the innate nature of the human soul, even when it is living in connection with the physical human body. After dissociating from the body and going to the spiritual world the soul remains the same. In other great religions of the world that is called "Intaqal", meaning "transfer" from this physical world to the spiritual realm. In the Bahá'í Faith this is called ascension to the lofty Kingdom of God; in the Hindu religious terminology it is called "Swargarohan", meaning "ascension to Paradise." There is no death between any two births. It is simply birth after birth. The idea of putting the word "death" in between the two births is a relative latecomer in Hindu literature.

In God's Maya, the Manifestation of God, His devotees, friends, enemies, foolish people and all other categories of persons collectively appear in sequence and play their respective roles in the same basic way as in the previous religious dispensations. This is called the reincarnation of qualities and rebirth of attributes. This, though similar, is called the "same", and this is the root cause of misunderstanding.

Last year's mango and this year's mango, even from the same tree or the same branch, are absolutely different from one another, yet, if we call them both the "same", keeping in view their essential qualities, it is not wrong. Shastras call the son as a reincarnation of his father if he represents the same behaviour and similar attributes in life.

An industrial concern manufactures several items. Each item includes many pieces. We call them the "same". Not only this, but we emphatically call them "exactly the same" whether produced this year or even ten years ago because each piece is standardised in quality and nature. Each mold, moulds thousands of pieces of some particular thing, and the pieces are called exactly the same. But in reality, each piece is not exactly the "same" because, among other things, it is made up of different atoms.

Thus we see that reincarnation of similar qualities and rebirth of similar attributes in people can take place, but they cannot be exactly the same. Both in outward appearance and inward character there has never been, there is not, nor will there ever be a person exactly like you in this world.

Now we shall refer specifically to the aspect of the return, renewal, resurrection of divine revelation through the reappearance of the Manifestation of God in each age. This takes place in the form of the reappearance of the divine attributes and the heavenly qualities in the life and teachings of the Founder of a religion each time. Many people are prone to mix this up with their ideas of reincarnation or transmigration of individual souls from body to body.

What is taught by the Holy Revelation is as follows:

......Endeavour to grasp the significance of "return", "revelation", and "resurrection", as witnessed in the days of the Manifestations of the divine Essence, that thou mayest behold with thine own eyes the "return" of the holy souls into sanctified and illumined bodies, and mayest wash away the dust of ignorance, and cleanse the darkened self with the waters of mercy flowing from the Source of divine Knowledge; that perchance thou mayest, through the power of God and the light of divine guidance, distinguish the Morn of everlasting splendour from the darksome night of error.

Furthermore, it is evident to thee that the Bearers of the trust of God are made manifest unto the peoples of the earth as the Exponents of a new Cause and the Bearers of a new Message. Inasmuch as these Birds of the Celestial Throne are all sent down from the heaven of the Will of God, and as they all arise to proclaim His irresistible Faith, they therefore are regarded as one soul and the same person. For they all drink from the one cup of the love of God, and all partake of the fruit of the same Tree of Oneness.

[Bahá'u'lláh, *The Kitáb-i-íqán; The Book of Certitude, pp. 97-98*]

This "Tree of Oneness" is called in the holy *Gita* "Ashvattha-Vriksha":

ऊर्ध्वमूलमधः शाखमश्वत्थं प्राहुरव्ययम् ।
छन्दांसि यस्य पर्णानि यस्तं वेद स वेदवित् ॥

अधश्चोर्ध्वं प्रसृतास्तस्य शाखा गुणप्रवृद्धा विषयप्रवाताः ।
अधश्च मूलान्यनुसंततानि कर्मानुबन्धीनि मनुष्य लोके ॥

[गीता 15: 1-2]

The Mighty Lord said:

"The imperishable Ashvattha Tree is said to be with its roots above and branches below; its leaves are the mantras (verses) of the Vedas and he who knows it is the knower of the Vedas.

Its branches are spread below and above, nourished by the attributes, sense-objects are its buds, and the roots stretch downwards in the world of men binding with action."

[Gita XV, 1-2]

As in the case of the appearance and return of Lord Krishna, the appearance of a Manifestation of God age after age in this world of humanity has its roots above in the Supreme Heaven of the Will of Lord Vishnu, the Unmanifest God, Who sends forth His Manifestation in every age with a new divine revelation, the teachings of which are progressive in accordance with the increasing spiritual capacities of human beings. The Holy Verses each Manifestation of God reveals may be termed the Vedas, which means the Knowledge of Divine Doctrine. Such holy revelations have spread their branches, in various parts of the human world, and are actually nourishing divine attributes in human beings. In practical life, they strengthen spiritual intelligence to control bodily senses in all worldly activities. They bind the people together in unity.

Thus we see that The Avatar has a dual station. Firstly he is the return of the spirit of Lord Vishnu. Secondly he is a human form bound by the senses and physical laws. He is thus an example of the spiritual Reality for all mankind. He is also the cause of the spread of spiritual inspiration. The Divine spirit returns from age to age. The human form is different each time.

Now as regards the rebirth and return of Arjuna, the foremost follower of Lord Krishna, let us understand the spiritual significance of the rebirth of the devoted followers of the Manifestation of God. In the words of Bahá'u'lláh:

......Whoever believed in Him (the Manifestation of God) and acknowledged His Faith, was endowed with the grace of a new life. Of him it would be truly said that he was reborn and revived, inasmuch as previous to his belief in God and his acceptance of His Manifestation, he had set his affections on the things of the world, such as attachment to earthly goods, to wife, children, food, drink, and the like, so much so that in the day-time and in the night season his one concern had been to amass riches and procure for himself the means of enjoyment and pleasure. Aside from these things, before his partaking of the reviving waters of faith, he had been so wedded to the traditions of his forefathers, and so passionately devoted to the observance of their customs and laws, that he would have preferred to suffer death rather than violate one letter of those superstitious forms and manners current amongst his people. Even as the people have cried: "Verily we found our fathers with a faith, and verily, in their footsteps we follow." (1)

---

1. Qur'án 43:22

"These same people, though wrapt in all these veils of limitation, and despite the restraint of such observances, as soon as they drank the immortal draught of faith, from the cup of certitude, at the hand of the Manifestation of the All-Glorious, were so transformed that they would renounce for His sake their kindred, their substance, their lives, their beliefs, yea, all else save God! So overpowering was their yearning for God, so uplifting their transports of ecstatic delight, that the world and all that is therein faded before their eyes into nothingness. Have not this people exemplified the mysteries of "rebirth" and "return"? Hath it not been witnessed that these same people, ere they were endued with the new and wondrous grace of God, sought through innumerable devices, to ensure the protection of their lives against destruction? Would not a thorn fill them with terror, and the sight of a fox put them to flight? But once having been honoured with God's supreme distinction and having been vouchsafed His bountiful grace, they would, if they were able, have freely offered up ten thousand lives in His path! Nay, their blessed souls, contemptuous of the cage of their bodies, would yearn for deliverance. A single warrior of that host would face and fight a multitude! And yet, how could they, but for the transformation wrought in their lives, be capable of manifesting such deeds which are contrary to the ways of men and incompatible with their worldly desires?

It is evident that nothing short of this mystic transformation could cause such spirit and behaviour, so utterly unlike their previous habits and manners, to be made manifest in the world of being. For their agitation was turned into peace, their doubt into certitude, their timidity into courage. Such is the potency of the Divine

Elixir, which, swift as the twinkling of an eye, transmuteth the souls of men!

For instance, consider the substance of copper. Were it to be protected in its own mine from becoming solidified, it would, within the space of seventy years, attain to the state of gold. There are some, however, who maintain that copper itself is gold, which by becoming solidified is in a diseased condition, and hath not therefore reached its own state.

Be that as it may, the real elixer will, in one instant, cause the substance of copper to attain the state of gold, and will traverse the seventy-year stages in a single moment. Could this gold be called copper? Could it be claimed that it hath not attained the state of gold, whilst the touchstone is at hand to assay it and distinguish it from copper?

Likewise, these souls through the potency of the Divine Elixir, traverse, in the twinkling of an eye, the world of dust and advance into the realm of holiness; and with one step cover the earth of limitations and reach the domain of the Placeless. It behoveth thee to exert thine utmost to attain unto this Elixir which, in one fleeting breath, causeth the west of ignorance to reach the east of knowledge, illuminates the darkness of night with the resplendence of the morn, guideth the wanderer in the wilderness of doubt to the well-spring of the Divine Presence and Pount of certitude, and conferreth upon mortal souls the honour of acceptance into the Ridván of immortality. Now, could this gold be thought to be copper, these people could likewise be thought to be the same as before they were endowed with faith.

O brother, behold how the inner mysteries of "rebirth", of "return", and of "resurrection" have each, through these all-sufficing, these unanswerable, and conclusive utterances, been unveiled and unravelled before thine eyes. God grant that through His gracious and invisible assistance, thou mayest divest thy body and soul of the old garment, and array thyself with the new and imperishable attire.

Therefore, those who in every subsequent Dispensation preceded the rest of mankind in embracing the Faith of God, who quaffed the clear waters of knowledge at the hand of the divine Beauty, and attained the loftiest summits of faith and certitude, these can be regarded, in name, in reality, in deeds, in words, and in rank, as the "return" of those who in a former Dispensation had achieved similar distinctions. For whatsoever the people of a former Dispensation have manifested, the same hath been shown by the people of this latter generation. Consider the rose: whether it blossometh in the East or in the West, it is none the less a rose. For what mattereth in this respect is not the outward shape and form of the rose, but rather the smell and fragrance which it doth impart."

[Bahá'u'lláh, *The Kitáb-i-íqán; The Book of Certitude, pp. 99-102*]

CHAPTER FOUR

It is thus clear that the attributes of the Manifestation of God, and His near and dear ones return once again to this planet. Once more religion is reborn and the universal cycle is repeated.

An incident from the early history of the Bahá'í Faith illustrates this concept of rebirth, of coming again. This occurred in the early 1900's in Haifa, Israel the World Centre of the Bahá'í Faith.

"Narayenrao Rangnath Shethji (1886-1943), known as Vakil, was the first Bahá'í among the Hindu nation. He had been raised as an orthodox Hindu and as a devotee of Lord Krishna, but he came to accept that Bahá'u'lláh, who was the return of Lord Krishna, had come to the world to bring unity to the religions of mankind. Vakil was betrothed to a young girl, Jashodaben (1904-1966), who was a Hindu. While on his first pilgrimage to the Holy Land, where Bahá'u'lláh had spent the last years of His life as a prisoner and an exile, Vakil asked 'Abdu'l-Bahá about his prospective marriage. 'Abdu'l-Bahá replied, "Marry the girl to whom you are betrothed and I pray that she may become a Bahá'í..."

[Dipchand Khianra, *Immortals, p. 14*]

In 1929, Vakil went on pilgrimage to the Holy Land again, but this time he was accompanied by his wife Jashodaben and two lovely daughters. By that time 'Abdu'l-Bahá had passed on to the next world (in 1921) and had appointed His grandson Shoghi Effendi as the Guardian of the Bahá'í Faith. The Guardian showered love and kindness on the whole family.

"Jashodaben had always been a great devotee of Lord Krishna and, although she loved her husband and was a good wife to him, she did not share his beliefs.

While in the Holy Land, she spent much time with the Greatest Holy Leaf (the daughters of Bahá'u'lláh and sister of 'Abdu'l-Bahá) who was the kindest and sweetest person she had ever known. There was a woman there who knew Gujarati and translated for her and her children.

Jashodaben continued with her own prayers and worship of Lord Krishna until one night when the Guardian sent the family to sleep in the Mansion of Bahá'u'lláh in Bahjí. Before going to bed, Jashodaben said her prayers as usual and put the Holy Book *Bhagavad Gita* with a picture of Lord Krishna under her pillow. That night Jashodaben had a beautiful dream. She saw a holy Figure in white standing by a cupboard from which he took out beautiful jewelled crowns, one after the other, and gave them to her to put in another cupboard in the room. Every crown was more beautiful than the other, and the holy Figure said to her that these were the crowns of Lord Krishna which now belonged to Bahá'u'lláh. Then she saw Lord Krishna and Bahá'u'lláh together. Lord Krishna took off his crown and gave it to Bahá'u'lláh, and Bahá'u'lláh gave His *Taj** to Lord Krishna. Bahá'u'lláh then looked at Jashodaben and said, "There is no difference between us; we are the same."

---

* Taj literally means crown. It is a headgear which Bahá'u'lláh used to wear.

The next morning Jashodaben woke up very happy and narrated her dream to her husband. Vakil's joy was boundless because he knew that the words of 'Abdu'l-Bahá had now become true and his wife had become a Bahá'í.

Even before she was a believer in this Cause, 'Abdu'l-Bahá had mentioned Jashodaben in His Tablets (letters) to her husband....

In 1919, 'Abdu'l-Bahá addressed a Tablet to both Vakil and his wife in which He said:

"O two candles of Divine Love!.....I pray in the Court of Oneness for you to be guarded and protected under His guard and protection, and to be helped in propagating the verses of Unity and assisted in guiding others, so that you may lay a foundation of everlasting life in this perishable world and kindle a light in this darkness of the physical kingdom..."
[Dipchand Khianra, *Immortals, pp. 27-29*]

We can therefore see that the recognition of truth irrespective of name, culture, creed or class is based on both reason and understanding as well as on Faith and emotion. Both these faculties must be in unity and harmony. Only then will the light of Faith be protected by the lamp of reason. For the individuals growth both are required.

Bahá'ís believe that Bahá'u'lláh has brought a new divine revelation suited to the needs of the modern age. He gives the most fundamental teaching of the existence of God whose essence is an incomprehensible mystery. The basic purpose of man is to know and love God. This capacity to know and love God is ".... the generating impulse and the primary purpose underlying the whole of creation." (Bahá'u'lláh, *Gleanings from the Writings of Bahá'u'lláh, XXVII*). The knowledge and love of God are sought not only because they are qualities necessary in this life but also because they are needed in the spiritual world to come. The purpose of life on this earth is to develop the good qualities needed in the wonderful world to come. 'Abdu'l-Bahá declared,

> *"What is he in need of in the Kingdom which transcends the life and limitation of this mortal sphere? That world beyond is a world of sanctity and radiance; therefore it is necessary that in this world he should acquire these divine attributes. In that world there is need of spirituality, faith, assurance, the knowledge and love of God. These he must attain in this world so that after his ascension from the earthly to the heavenly Kingdom he shall find all that is needful in that life eternal ready for him."*
>
> ['Abdu'l-Bahá, *Foundations of World Unity*, p. 63]

God is manifested and made known to man through His Manifestations, those great souls possessed of the Holy Spirit, the central Figures of the world's great religions. Some appeared in the world in such ancient times that Their names have been lost. But others are well known today. They include such mighty figures as Sri Rama, Lord Krishna, the Buddha, Lord Abraham, Lord Moses, Lord Zoroaster, Jesus the Christ, the Prophet Muhammád, and in this age, the Báb (the forerunner of Bahá'u'lláh), and Bahá'u'lláh. In the Bahá'í Writings the unity of the Manifestations of God and the singleness of their purpose are upheld. There is only one religion of God. This one religion is progressive. Differences in beliefs of the peoples of the world must not lead to conflict. All the Manifestations are like teachers in the same school of this world. Here the religion of God is taught. This school has different classes according to each era and different teachers for each class or age. All the teachers are united in their purpose and teach the students (mankind) what is needed, each according to the capacity of their class.

It is evident that God provides guidance to mankind not only for the spiritual development of the individual but for society as a whole. It is now up to each person to achieve what he or she is capable of doing. After toiling on this planet and passing through each of the various stages the individual soul will leave its physical body behind and pass on to a spiritual realm. Here it will be conscious of what it has achieved and will receive its reward or punishment. It will continue its journey to God in whatever state or form is appropriate but always aware and growing from stage to stage.

Thus though we may be unable to understand the nature and details of the world's to come because of our lack of spiritual understanding, we are assured that happiness is the goal of our life. We can look forward to an eternity of Grace and Mercy and Joy. This is our incentive to honest work and service in the path of God. This is the purpose of God's creation!

As old superstitions and blind beliefs are swept away throughout the world and throughout India and new patterns of life come into being suited to the modern age, we can look forward, in the long run, to a very bright future for mankind and for the masses of India. But we must work unitedly toward that end. India and its people will be given a new life when the age-old beliefs associated with the theory of reincarnation and the transmigration of souls are replaced by new beliefs suited to modern man. The task is an enormous one and will continue for many years to come. But the world does not stand still. India can become a paradise.

NOTE

Dr. H.M. Munje was an outstanding teacher of the Bahá'í Faith and a member of the National Spiritual Assembly of the Bahá'ís of India for over 40 years. He was a highly accomplished homeopathic doctor, and the founder of a college of homeopathy in Kanpur, Uttar Pradesh. He was the author of other books including *The Whole World is But One Family* and *1844 : Pinpoint Target of All Faiths.*

Dr. Munje died at the age of 78 just before completing the first draft of the manuscript for this book. His daughter, Dr. (Mrs.) Radha Munje Rost, and her husband, Dr. H.T.D. Rost, undertook to complete the task. They had discussed the manuscript with him at great length, often going far into the night, when it was being written in the late 1980s and therefore had a clear idea of his approach, views, and intentions. In completing the work Dr. H.T.D. Rost wrote the section on "near-death experiences" at Dr. Munje's request, the whole of chapter 4, and bits and pieces of the rest of the final manuscript. Dr. Radha Rost checked the primary Sanskrit sources and made many valuable alterations and improvements. But the book is basically a product of Dr. Munje's experience, knowledge, and will.

Dr. Munje was knowledgeable in 14 languages and had made a deep study of the world's great religions from childhood, often being able to read the sacred texts in the original languages. He had a deep knowledge of Sanskrit. Referring to "The Reincarnation Mystery Revealed", Dr. Munje wrote, "This is my laborious and difficult fifty years of research work through my in-depth study of the Hindu Scriptures in their original Sanskrit texts."

[Letter from Dr. H.M. Munje to
Mr. A.A. Furutan, March 29]

A professor of Sanskrit at Fergusson College, Pune, highly praised a translation Dr. Munje had made of a Bahá'í Holy Book, The Hidden Words of Bahá'u'lláh, into Sanskrit. The professor declared that the book read like the Vedas.

Dr. Munje not only studied the holy texts on the subject of reincarnation extensively, but also explained to Dr. and Dr. (Mrs.) Rost that he discussed it with Hindu pundits, priests, and holy men over a period of many years. He said that the very passages from the sacred books that the priests used to try to prove the validity of the theory of reincarnation, as Hindus commonly understand it, are used by him in this book in this endeavor to show that it is invalid.

This is very challenging, difficult, and complex subject. It is hoped that justice has been done in presenting Dr. Munje's views as he would have wished. *The Reincarnation Mystery Revealed* is certainly not going to be the last word on the subject of reincarnation. But surely this historic book reveals new insights into the subject that challenge a multitude of sometimes contradictory, inadequately supported, and occasionally even unexamined suppositions.